TOMMY MURPHY is is a graduate of the National Institute of Dramatic Art (Director's Course). His plays for young people are *Troy's House* (1998), *Precipice* (2007) and an adaptation of Marlowe's *Massacre at Paris* (2001). In 2005 *Strangers in Between* premiered at Griffin Theatre Company, where Tommy was writer-in-residence, winning the NSW Premier's Literary Award and subsequently touring nationally in 2008. His adaptation of Timothy Conigrave's memoir *Holding the Man* premiered at Griffin Theatre Company in 2006. It won the NSW Premier's Literary Award, the 2007 Australian Writers' Guild Award (AWGIE) and the Philip Parsons Young Playwright's Award. It was remounted for the 2007 Sydney Mardi Gras Festival before transferring to Sydney Opera House, Company B Belvoir, Melbourne Theatre Company and Brisbane Powerhouse. It was produced in San Francisco by the New Conservatory Theatre Centre and a new production opened on London's West End in April 2010. *Saturn's Return* premiered at the Sydney Theatre Company Wharf 2 in 2008 and transferred to the main stage in 2009. Tommy is a past president of Sydney University Dramatic Society and a current board member of Australian Theatre for Young People.

Melissa Jaffer as Gwen in the 2010 Company B / La Boite production in Sydney. (Photo: Heidrun Löhr)

GWEN in PURGATORY

a play by
TOMMY MURPHY

CURRENCY PRESS
SYDNEY

CURRENCY PLAYS

First published in 2010
by Currency Press Pty Ltd,
PO Box 2287, Strawberry Hills, NSW, 2012, Australia
enquiries@currency.com.au
www.currency.com.au

Second edition.

NATIONAL LIBRARY OF AUSTRALIA CIP DATA

Author:	Murphy, Tommy.
Title:	Gwen in Purgatory / Tommy Murphy.
Edition:	2nd ed.
ISBN:	9780868198941 (pbk.)
Subjects:	Australian drama–21st century.
Dewey Number:	A822.4

Typeset by Dean Nottle for Currency Press.
Printed by Hyde Park Press, Richmond, SA.
Cover design by Emma Vine, Currency Press.
Front cover shows Melissa Jaffer.
Cover photograph by Michael Corridore.

Contents

Melissa Jaffer as Gwen and Nathaniel Dean as Daniel in the 2010 Company B / La Boite production in Sydney. (Photo: Heidrun Löhr)

Introduction

Tommy was born the year after I'd left Sydney University Dramatic Society and begun my professional career up the road at Nimrod in what is now the Belvoir St Theatre. I mention this in part as a sentimental tribute to that singular institution called SUDS that nurtured both of us a generation apart. SUDS was a formidable place of dreams; we came from our high schools with our fears and our instincts and desires, seeking the like-minded, and we were formed somehow for life. The parties were very good but so were the opportunities for making theatre: far from the reach of academics or coursework, we were there creating our own paths, finding out what worked in our own terms, beginning to form a sense of what is known as 'technique'.

I was lucky enough to catch Tommy's 1999 play *Troy's House* in the Cellar Theatre at Sydney Uni—the first of his plays with SUDS. With something of a debt to *The Young Ones*, perhaps, the play looked at a share student household in Canberra. It was fresh, funny and playful, but most impressive of all was its assurance—it knew what it was.

Tommy grew up in Queanbeyan, fifteen kilometres from Canberra, the seventh of eight children in what was, we can assume, a noisy, loving and, it goes without saying, Catholic family. His plays draw a great energy from his ingrained understanding of the comedy, contradictions and needs of a life lived outside a metropolitan community.

In his breakthrough play *Strangers in Between* (2005) Tommy takes a character from the country and brings him into the city. It was the necessary working out in theatrical form of Tommy's own shift to Sydney. As a writer, he was off and running.

Spinning with confidence and playful theatricality, his adaptation of Tim Conigrave's memoir *Holding the Man* (2006) casts its net across a whole era and brilliantly tells a profoundly moving tale of life and love. In *Saturn's Return* (2008) Tommy experiments with form further, fragmenting narrative and playing with the theatrical identity of character.

But in *Gwen in Purgatory* Tommy was determined to return to the source: to Queanbeyan. He embraced certain formal principles from the start. He knew, for instance, that the play would happen in 'real time'—a significant departure as all his previous work displays a more cinematic structure: relatively brief scenes that play their moment and then 'cut' forward to propel the story. In *Gwen* Tommy has his leading lady in her chair, and nothing interrupts or offers an escape from this purgatorial imprisonment—well, nothing except the need to pop off to the bedroom and slip into her tennis gear!

It has been a privilege to watch Tommy, over the past two years, harness his ideas for *Gwen* and follow his instincts with such clarity and determination. I have simply listened, mostly in silence, and watched this play take on flesh.

Or rather, take on bone. Because Tommy always had the flesh. What wasn't there was the structural framework to support it. In fact he deliberately resisted imposing 'story' too soon. In this, his process is really the reverse of how most playwrights seem to construct a play. He has the characters and, in this instance, the house and the room in which they meet, but the skeleton of action has been developed through months and months of work, frequently with actors reading and discussing, sometimes with Tommy, me or dramaturg Eamon Flack reading to each other, mostly with Tommy at his computer with his cat Narelle.

It has been a lovely period of rehearsal. In the way of these things, the cast has formed deep bonds and the fictional relationships in the play are being reinforced and re-rehearsed in the relationships between the actors in rehearsal and in dressing-room. This is the way of the theatre.

Tommy knows this world, knows these people, and this confidence has granted him the licence to make the symbolic exaggerations that characterise this play. This is a home without sustenance: the fridge is empty, the kettle is never found, the slice is never made. I love the formal device by which the observer, Father Ezekiel, denied his sabbatical in New York or London, lands in Queanbeyan and provides the frame through which we observe the currents of this particular Irish-Catholic inheritance. Meanwhile, a world away, his mother sits on a bus winding its way along dangerous roads to the office in Lagos that boasts a computer with Skype.

Tommy's great theme is *home*. He is blessed with a profound under-standing of the dynamics of family. In rehearsal he was often at pains to point out that, while we were getting carried away with the exploration of subtext, this is a play about what people do to each other out of love. 'There's enough drama in kindness,' he would say, 'enough disaster in simply trying to do the right thing'.

The road to hell is, after all, paved with good intentions.

All the actors who've come near this play have made a difference. Melissa Jaffer, Nat Dean, Pacharo Mzembe, Sue Ingleton and Grant Dodwell have all been amazing. I'd also like to thank the actors who participated in our workshops: Lynette Curran, Aaron Davison, Jack Finsterer, Julie Forsyth, Russell Kiefel, Steve le Marquand, Dorian Nkono, Rebecca Massey and Steve Rodgers. And I want to pay tribute to our dear Monica Maughan, whose life journey coincided, for a while, with the journey of this play.

Neil Armfield
Sydney, October 2010

Neil Armfield is a director of theatre, film and opera. He is Artistic Director of Company B Belvoir in Sydney. He directed the premiere season of *Gwen in Purgatory* in 2010.

Playwright's Note

I am remembering now that my original proposal to Company B Belvoir was to write a play dealing, somehow, with memory. At the time I was reeling from the recent news that someone close to me would lose their memory. As sometimes happens, these real life circumstances were too raw so I let the play evolve in a new direction. The character suffering from memory loss was not granted his entrance beyond the first draft. I focussed my attention instead on the other figures that were beginning to populate my play. But a fascination with memory seems to have remained.

Science and literature have long struggled to explain memory. Plato's image of memory as a wax tablet remains in our language today when we describe 'impressions'. These attempted analogies shift with the advent of technology; perhaps memory is like the computer I am typing on right now, or the voice recorder from which I am transcribing these words. But, of course, as I type, I am tampering with the words. How do we account for memory as the reconstruction of life replete with the unreliability, the subjectivity, the editing, the colouring and the exaggerations? How do we describe recollection as a creative act?

Memory is like writing a play.

After about a year of writing, something clicked in the story and I was surprised to discover that much of the play is in fact underpinned by disputed memories. Perhaps this is a likely conflict in a family, among people who may have opposing interpretations of their shared history and shared identity.

The voices in this play stem from people I know and love but as soon as they found their way to the page they were characters bending according to dramatic impulses and artistic imperatives. Now that they reach the stage, the characters are merely impressions of those inspiring people. A play is a rectified account of life.

That said, I do know a beautiful woman who played her last game of tennis in her backyard court at age ninety. I have also encountered people fearful that they will find themselves in a kind of purgatory, abandoned by family at the cruellest moment, the twilight of life. I have interviewed priests from developing nations, several from Nigeria, who like Father Ezekiel have been brought to Australia to fill the gap left by dwindling priest recruits. They expressed feelings of isolation and regret for the 'individualism' of Australia. They seemed homesick for a church that relishes greater influence over its community. To me these missionaries stand for the church's resistance of bigger questions about its place in Australian society.

And with that, I welcome you to Queanbeyan, the town that was there first before they built the nation's capital up the road. It is a place I will never forget...

Tommy Murphy
Sydney, October 2010

For my mother and my grandmother

PLAYWRIGHT'S THANKS

Firstly I would like to thank Eamon Flack and Neil Armfield for their patient dramaturgy. I am also grateful for the guidance provided by Leo Butler, Ruth Little and my fellow playwrights in the Royal Court Young Writers' Program, which I attended via the generous assistance of the British Council. Several organisations provided me a space to write this play at various times including The Royal Court, Paines Plough Theatre, The Bush Theatre, The Bundanon Trust and The Faculty of Education and Social Work at The University of Sydney where I am an Honorary Associate. The actors who workshopped this play were: Lynette Curran, Aaron Davison, Jack Finsterer, Julie Forsyth, Russell Kiefel, Steve le Marquand, Dorian Nkono, Rebecca Massey, Steve Rodgers and the premiere cast. I would also like to pay tribute to the late Monica Maughan. Other people who assisted with the research and creation of this play include Father Constantine Osuchukwa; Brother Bob Wallace cfc AM; Father John Mutuku; Father Magnus Kobbi; Father Andrew Mutubusi; Father Biju Joseph Puthenpura; Father Michael SungJae Hwang; Michael Slattery, Clergy Liaison and Formation Broken Bay Diocese; Dr Steven Lovell-Jones, Executive Officer to the Chancellor & Justice & Peace Promoter Catholic Archdiocese of Sydney; Father Peter Day; David Berthold at La Boite Theatre Company; Penguin Plays Rough; Antonia Aitken; Ross Byers; Hugh O'Keefe; Schuyler Weis; Lucy Wirth; Cathy Hunt; Kate and Paddy Murphy; Dane Crawford; Patricia and Philip Murphy; Elsa O'Malley.

TM

Gwen in Purgatory was first produced by Company B Belvoir and La Boite Theatre at Belvoir St Upstairs Theatre, Sydney, on 4 August 2010, with the following cast:

DANIEL	Nathaniel Dean
LAURIE	Grant Dodwell
PEG	Sue Ingleton
GWEN	Melissa Jaffer
FATHER EZEKIEL	Pacharo Mzembe

Director, Neil Armfield
Set Designer, Stephen Curtis
Costume Designer, Bruce McKinven
Lighting Designer, David Walters
Sound Designer, Paul Charlier
Dramaturg, Eamon Flack
Assistant Director, Cristabel Sved
Rehearsal Observer, Dino Dimitriadis
Stage Manager, Mark Lowrey
Assistant Stage Manager, Sophie Baker

CHARACTERS

GWEN, 90
DANIEL, 32
FATHER EZEKIEL, 28
PEG, 65
LAURIE, 59

GWEN *is at home, almost.*

The room is brand spanking new with an open-plan kitchen and tiled floor. Boxes remain unpacked and Gwen's new dining table is wrapped in protective plastic. A rolling pin and some baking utensils remain Mary-Celeste-like on the bench.

GWEN *is waiting in her Sunday best, a stylish homemade outfit. She is attentive to the goings-on around her. There is seemingly nothing going on around her. Don't sleep,* GWEN. *Don't sleep,* GWEN. *Don't sleep,* GWEN. *Dip by dip,* GWEN *ebbs into shallow sleep.*

The phone rings! GWEN *soon computes where she is and what is alarming her. The phone. She does her preparation for standing, gaining sufficient momentum, up, steady, and finally she can shuffle. She is but a few steps from her chair when the phone stops.* GWEN *stops. She'll sit again.*

As soon as GWEN *is seated, the phone rings. The standing regime repeated,* GWEN *moves as fast as her frame of ninety years will carry her: it's not a run and not much quicker than her walk, but her arms move more.*

The phone stops when GWEN *is achingly close. Bending is a strain, but* GWEN *picks up the phone. Ignorant of the benefit of a cordless,* GWEN *carts the entire apparatus back to her chair. The cord follows, freeing itself from the socket.*

GWEN *sits and waits for the disconnected phone to ring. A phone rings.* GWEN *answers the phone on her lap.*

GWEN: Hello. Hello?

> GWEN *does not see the ringing mobile on the bench behind her.*

Are you there? Can you speak up? Hang on, the cord's out.

> GWEN *places the landline phone on her chair and pushes it all to the socket. It isn't easy but she manages to reconnect the phone, collect the user's manual and sit in her chair. She'll wait again.*

> GWEN *opens the user's manual. Her eyes strain. Where are her reading glasses? They are on a distant box. She stands. The phone rings. She answers.*

Sorry about that. It wasn't plugged in. How can I help you?

But it's not this phone that's ringing, GWEN; *it's that one over on the bench. She notices the ringing mobile now. The race is on. As* GWEN *hurries to the ringing mobile she sees that she might actually make it. Her hand is about to touch the mobile when it stops. Never mind.* GWEN *returns to her seat armed with all of the controls, the phones, her reading glasses and the user's manual. She sits.*

Doorbell.

GWEN *stands. The doorbell chimes again and again on her approach. She slows. Someone bangs at the door. She halts. Someone is moving around the house, peering in windows. The menacing shape of a man at the glass has* GWEN *backing towards her phone. Another knock.* GWEN*'s hand is trembling as she holds the phone and tries to call a number. The phone rings in her hand and she throws it down. She turns to the other phone and it rings. She answers it.*

Yes. Who? Oh. I'm scared half to death in here. Yes. Oh, will I let you in? Yes. Wait a minute while I find my key. Yes. I'm getting the key. You're at my door. Yes. Come to the front door. I know. I have the key. I'm no good with the locks in this place. It's like— My old place had— It's like Fort Knox. Pardon? Yes. I'm going to let you in. No. Fort Knox. I'm doing it. I've got myself a new phone but I'm no— Yes but I didn't— Yes. No. Fort Knox. You're not hearing me. The United States Bullion Depository. Will you wait till I— Yes. Yes. Hang on. I'm no good with—

The door opened—

Thank heavens it's only you.

DANIEL, GWEN*'s grandson is at the door. He wears a 'high vis' fluorescent work jacket.*

DANIEL: Yeah. He's gone.
GWEN: Who's gone?
DANIEL: That bloke. He's long gone.
GWEN: I know he's long gone. I saw him go.
DANIEL: What are y'worried about? He's not coming back.
GWEN: What are you doing calling from the front yard?

DANIEL: Checking you're okay.

GWEN: Come to the door then.

DANIEL: I did. You okay?

GWEN: I'm wonderful.

DANIEL: You didn't answer.

GWEN: I thought you'd gone too.

DANIEL: I called from up the road but you didn't answer so I came back.

GWEN: I didn't know who this was at my door.

DANIEL: It was just me.

GWEN: Well that's clear now, Mark.

DANIEL: Daniel.

GWEN: Daniel. I mean Daniel. You grandkids, you're all the image of each other. Are you staying?

DANIEL: Nah, I'm going.

GWEN: But will you come inside this time? Come in, Daniel.

DANIEL: D'you know how to answer that mobile phone, Nana?

GWEN: Phones phones.

DANIEL: Y'right?

GWEN: No it is good when they all call. I'm alright. I'm teaching myself to use this phone Naomi bought me but I'll need someone to organise the cords. I've read the manual to the air conditioner—

DANIEL: Okay—

GWEN: I've read the manual to the air conditioner and the oven but it was that hot here last night I thought—

DANIEL: You'd confused them.

GWEN: I said, I've gone and used the—

DANIEL: Air conditioner for—

GWEN: No, I've used the oven manual for the air conditioner and I'm roasting myself alive.

DANIEL: Yeah.

GWEN: Is what I said, what I thought to myself—maybe I said it out loud. Dear I laughed. Yes.

DANIEL: Well, glad you're alright.

GWEN: Yes, well, I've got the air conditioner sorted and you won't be interested in an oven but the new microwave… See I did a class when they came in—take a seat—and they all said, oh well, that we'd be only using microwaves and that sort of thing. The future. I went to the Tech because even Margaret Fulton said it but no I'll use it for beverages. I'll use it for AktaVite and a tea that's been sitting. Heat up a meal. Steam vegetables. Oh, jacket potato. Would you like a cup of tea?

DANIEL: I'll get a bought coffee later.

GWEN: They'll only make you pay for a bought coffee, Daniel.

DANIEL: Yeah but I like shop coffee.

GWEN: I'd have to get you to unpack the kettle. Take a seat. I insisted on keeping my old enamel kettle.

DANIEL: You should have called me.

GWEN: I did call you. I found your number in my teledex.

DANIEL: For the move. It would have been cheaper. I have a truck.

GWEN: I had these professionals come in. They're very good. Kelly the Careful Carrier. He says he'll replace my cheese bell.

DANIEL: What's a cheese bell?

GWEN: Covers the cheese. Like a bell. Glass. A glass bell that covers cheese. A cheese bell. Too precious to be packed with a mixmaster but I don't make a fuss— Leave it, Daniel. Don't go shifting boxes. I'll only lose my bearings— Have a look around if you like.

DANIEL: They won't like it if they think I've knocked off for the afternoon.

GWEN: Well don't let me keep you. Take a seat. I had a wonderful first night. Slept like a little girl.

DANIEL: Did ya?

GWEN: Hmmm?

DANIEL: Did you sleep like a little girl?

GWEN: Here I did, yes. Very dark and peaceful. It's really the bush here really. Yes. Takes me back in a nice way to before street lights and all this. Give yourself a tour, Daniel: you'll want a look.

DANIEL: In there?

> DANIEL *exits*.

GWEN: Go on. Wander in. See there? Garage, sewing room—Naomi's getting me a treadmill but I said 'no'—laundry at the back. That lovely big spare room. It's a lovely big spare room.

> GWEN *sees that* DANIEL *has left. She waits, alone and patient again.*
> DANIEL *returns, leaving open the door through to the garage.*

DANIEL: Real good.

GWEN: Hmmm?

DANIEL: It's really good, Nana.

GWEN: Oh yes. They're all envious of my new place, don't you worry. Peg… Peg's keen to get in here herself.

DANIEL: Peg is?

GWEN: One day. One day. I'm in no rush. Your Uncle Laurie's putting a garden in, which will be quite spectacular. They've marked up a new bed for me. 'Jim's Mowing and Home…' oh it's… 'Landscaping Services'?

DANIEL: Sounds expensive. I'll getcha soil for free down there at the river in Pop's wheelbarrow.

GWEN: You haven't got time to be digging holes for me, Daniel.

DANIEL: Bel and me talked about a place like this. We'd like a place as good as this, all new and all. Eventually Bel and me. I'd like a place like this. Tiles are good for cleaning. Tiles. Like this.

GWEN: What's Peg been saying about the tiles?

DANIEL: Nothin'.

GWEN: It's very easy to criticise.

DANIEL: I barely talk to Peg.

GWEN: Well you should.

DANIEL: I know.

GWEN: Keep in touch. She's your mother.

DANIEL: Sure.

GWEN: It's lovely when you all call. You ought to tell Peg I like the gloss finish.

DANIEL: So do I.

GWEN: Alright then.

DANIEL: Yeah. Nana… you did clip that bloke's ute before.

GWEN: Your Aunt Naomi does rice in her microwave.

DANIEL: Right. Nana, there was a mark on his ute.

GWEN: What rot.

DANIEL: Coming out of your drive here—

GWEN: The cheek of him.

DANIEL: It's just, you probably don't know this driveway like the old driveway. This new street's narrow.

GWEN: Yes, no, very, very on top of all that.

DANIEL: But anyhow I've sorted it; I calmed him down. He's gone. And I didn't mean to rush off.

GWEN: I knew to call you, Ducky.

DANIEL: If I'm delivering, I'm always about. You can always call me, Nana.

GWEN: You're a saint, Ducky. Coming when I call today. You're the, it's like you're the knight, you're like a knight in shining, that is a bit like armour, it's a, like a knight, a knight's shining armour, that iridescent thing you've got on; you're a knight. A knight. You're a knight in shining armour.

DANIEL: Thanks.

GWEN: 'Fancy!' you said, 'Fancy… fancy, threatening an old lady at her house!'

DANIEL: Something like that.

GWEN: Don't you worry, he was none too… You said, 'Hey, you listen here, boyo, this is my grandmother and fancy you jolly well trying to', oh, 'harangue'?

DANIEL: I, I said, 'Have a heart…'

GWEN: This is it.

DANIEL: 'Have a heart, you C.'

GWEN: And he did see.

DANIEL: Yeah, no, I…

GWEN: Did you say an unseemly?

DANIEL: Ye… Yeah I did.

GWEN: I don't use language; I wouldn't have heard that.

DANIEL: But we laughed at him.

GWEN: Well didn't he look comic just backing off and off his high horse and, yes…

DANIEL: Yeah.

GWEN: Oh yes. I chuckled. I roared laughing when his face, his face soon changed complexion when you pulled up. Great strapping… thing. Your truck coming around the corner there.

DANIEL: Well, no, I came in a taxi, Nana.

GWEN: Taxi?

DANIEL: My truck's in the workshop so I came in a taxi today.

GWEN: Taxi? Jove. I didn't see that.

DANIEL: Bel's got the car. You're not that far from the depot. You sounded urgent.

GWEN: Pass me my purse. Taxi?

DANIEL: Was gonna catch the bus back.

GWEN: Where is my purse?

DANIEL: On the bench. You won't pay for me taxi.

GWEN: The bus doesn't service here yet. There's not even a seat at that bus stop, Daniel.

DANIEL: There is a seat, but no timetable.

GWEN: Well there might be a timetable but there's no bus yet. My house is the first to be built. You'd have a wait on your hands.

DANIEL: That's why I came back. Can I borrow y'car?

GWEN: Oh no. No, I'll spin you in.

DANIEL: If you're not too…

GWEN: Not too busy.

DANIEL: Not too shaken?

GWEN: If I get cold I've got the air conditioner.

DANIEL: Can probably wait a little while.

GWEN: We'll just wait for the priest to show.

DANIEL: Priest? What, is he coming here?

GWEN: At first, I was hoping you were him. 'That's strange,' I thought, 'he's early'. Not so early but then when you knocked like that I said, I sat here and said, 'Now that's not the priest knocking so hard. That can't be the priest *bashing* like that.'

DANIEL: I was only—

GWEN: It's on the news about terrible break-ins: people coming to grief, attacks, men with bats and, oh, jokers. They'd use a bedside lamp within reach. It doesn't worry me. You just try to take my television and the—oh other things they might steal, Daniel—Black and Decker or—whatsit…

DANIEL: Y'sure you're right to get back in the car?

GWEN: Oh they might be after food, just groceries in the fridge— desperate, Daniel. They might want, well, money. Jewellery. They won't find the kettle. Naomi's generously paid for this alarm, a home security hooter, and I've got that many codes in my head but you can change it, you just ring your children and ask. Your Uncle Laurie changed my bank pin—

DANIEL: I wouldn't tell Uncle Laurie your pin, Nana.

GWEN: And Naomi's done the home alarm code and now all the pins are my birth year—

DANIEL: Don't tell people your pin, Nana.

GWEN: 1920.

DANIEL: That's how they'd rob you, Nana.

GWEN: No no, this is why this chap demonstrated the alarm and, well, it is that loud, well, and it makes, it makes burglars nauseous. Naomi says, 'You'll only know they've been by the pools of sick, Mum': frightful, really.

DANIEL: So your old place sold. You do alright?

GWEN: Listen, you can't be racing around buying coffee. Find that kettle.

DANIEL: Do you want a tea?

GWEN: I'll wait for Father.

DANIEL: Which priest is it?

GWEN: The little one…

DANIEL: Beg y'pardon?

GWEN: Where's little…?

DANIEL: Mykaela?

GWEN: Mykaela.

DANIEL: Mykaela's home with Bel.

GWEN: You should bring her around from time to time.

DANIEL: I will.

GWEN: Lovely.

DANIEL: Is it the drunk one, Nana? The priest coming here.

GWEN: Ezekiel. From Kenya.

DANIEL: What happened to Father Mooney?

GWEN: Father Mooney? Prison.

DANIEL: Ah, and we've had a pretty good run with all that here.

GWEN: Working in the prisons—

DANIEL: Ah not…

GWEN: Actually, it's hard to keep track because now they move priests more and more. Like Father Kevin Lynch going to Goulburn to be Prison Chaplain. Father Kevin Lynch went to the prisons. Father Mooney is dead. Died, poor man. Yes. Drink got him. Yes.

DANIEL: Oh right.

GWEN: I've left my run too late to bake Father's rum'n'raisin. S'pose I'll have to get a man in to look at the oven. And I didn't quite make it to Woollies just now.

DANIEL: No.

GWEN: No.

DANIEL: Nana, the Holden's big. Maybe it's too big for you.

GWEN: My car was the first automatic transmission in Queanbeyan. There's the oven manual when you get a moment, Ducky.

DANIEL: They'll probably make you do a driving test soon.

GWEN: Laurie's very good at reminding me. And I wouldn't want anyone else to add to the stress because it is stressful, Daniel, a driving examination.

DANIEL: You've had it already then?

GWEN: But tell me, what's 'blind spot'?

DANIEL: Something your doctor said?

GWEN: In the car, this girl, she's from the place, sitting there marking me holding a, oh a... She has this thing in her hands. Keeps me up at night.

DANIEL: They're making you do another test are they?

GWEN: Dive into my purse. Show me my licence. They gave me a gold licence; that's got to count for something, Daniel.

DANIEL: Let me show ya, Nana. I drive for a living. I'll show you.

GWEN: What is it you're showing me?

DANIEL: Y' blind spot.

GWEN: I don't know what 'blind spot' is.

DANIEL: I'll show you.

GWEN: Goodo.

DANIEL: So say here you are...

GWEN: Yes. I am.

DANIEL: And you wanna merge.

GWEN: Well I do. Good.

DANIEL: And then—

GWEN: Yes.

DANIEL: And then put the indicator on.

GWEN: I check the mirror.

DANIEL: Check the mirror and if there's no-one...

GWEN: There's no-one.

DANIEL: Indicator.

GWEN: The blinker.

DANIEL: Yeah. Face straight ahead. Check the mirror but, for the gap you can't see, turn your head over your shoulder.

GWEN: How's that?

DANIEL: Can you turn your head further?

GWEN: That?

DANIEL: No further?

GWEN: No, that's it.

DANIEL: Well. That's not very much but—

GWEN: It's enough.

DANIEL: I'm coming through and you'll see me in y'side vision.

DANIEL *passes* GWEN *as a car in the next lane.*

GWEN: 'Peripheral vision' is the term you want. Keep coming, Ducky.

DANIEL: Still?

GWEN: Not yet.

DANIEL: Not yet?

GWEN: There.

DANIEL: You can see me here but I'm in front of you now, Nana.

GWEN: I've got you. Safe to turn?

DANIEL: Well, yeah but see—

GWEN: And if I do that in the test she can't mark me down. You've been very helpful, Daniel, thank you. No, after the priest, let's you and me, Daniel, go for a drive.

DANIEL: Nana. I just think—

GWEN: It'll build my confidence and you'll see there's no need to worry about me on the roads, Ducky.

DANIEL: Nana. If you fail your next test, Nana, it might be something that, just, you just live with, I reckon.

GWEN: I get a second attempt.

DANIEL: What if, Nana, what if you hit a kid? Killed a kid or something. You couldn't live with yourself.

Silence.

GWEN: We all love Father Ezekiel. A wonderful smile, big wonderful smile and wonderful sermons about just wonderful—and he's very approachable and… From Kenya. Some will say, 'Oh, we can't understand that Father Ezekiel', but, no, I understand him perfectly clearly, don't you worry. No, his ordination was at the cathedral and we all went out: Peg and I and people from the parish. Singing. And we brought his dear mother across from…

DANIEL: Africa.

GWEN: All the way from Africa to see this and I gave a few dollars. I made slice for the stall. We raised an air ticket and she came and it was very, very emotional, very… He's a good priest and here because God sent him. He had wanted a sabbatical in New York or London but we need priests at the Queanbeyan parish and 'Providence' is how he described it in the bulletin. And I said well, 'Where will God lead me, dear Jesus?' And here I am. He'll come here today to bless this place and we'll keep it quiet that I spent too much at, not Gerry Harvey, the other one, at, out at Fyshwick. DFO Warehouse? Too much. Yes, I do think highly of Father Ezekiel. A good man. Kenyan. Yes… as black as your hat.

DANIEL: Nana, that's a bit racist.

GWEN: Well everyone likes to have a go at me.

DANIEL: I don't.

GWEN: They all know best. Mine was the first automatic transmission in Queanbeyan, did I say that?

DANIEL: No.

GWEN: And you do know I'm playing tennis every third Wednesday of the month, but for the court coming down and so many of my friends being unavailable.

DANIEL: That's a shame it's all going, Nana.

GWEN: I don't drive at night.

DANIEL: Nah.

GWEN: Forty miles an hour in a school zone.

DANIEL: Yep.

GWEN: Passed that test alright.

DANIEL: Sure. Forty kilometres.

GWEN: You clearly don't think I should.

DANIEL: Only…

GWEN: I'll turn my head and I'll check the blinkin' mirror and, and I'll ignore the girl making marks on her, on her… Oh blast! Blast. What's the wretched thing called? In her hands.

DANIEL: I don't know.

GWEN: I've told your Uncle Laurie I'm determined to do the test. When I decide it's time, well… Providence can sort out the rest. Your Uncle Laurie has had his eye on the car.

DANIEL: Uncle Laurie?

GWEN: Mmm.

DANIEL: No, Nana, Pop promised the Holden to me. Sorry but… We worked on it together one afternoon and he told me that I could have it when he was done with it. Nah, sorry but that's what he said.

GWEN: I'm still using it, Daniel.

DANIEL: Yeah. Yeah. Funny but: that bingle bloke out front. What a thing, hey? And me, a hand like that [*gesturing*] to this bloke. Flinch.

GWEN: I did flinch.

DANIEL: No it was him flinching, Nana. It made us laugh. Laughed because I just did that, like that [*gesturing*], and it made him flinch. Funny. See me raise me, just raise my arm. That scrunch in the face, like that. All funny. Face and little noise like that.

GWEN: There was a comedian they used to have on the television.

DANIEL: Yeah?

GWEN: This comedian… oh… what's his name? Used to get hit with things.

DANIEL: Yeah? Funny?

GWEN: Yes. Terribly funny.

DANIEL: Yeah. It's easy to break into those old Holdens, Nana.

GWEN: You won't tell people about this bingle will you?

DANIEL: No.

GWEN: It's in the past. No need to mention it to anyone.

DANIEL: I promise, Nana. Just there's a few dings on the car. It needs someone to have a look at it.

GWEN: I'm a good driver, Daniel. I am.

DANIEL: No worries, Nana.

Silence.

I remember Pop broke down.

GWEN: Well… Maybe once or twice but I have it serviced now.

DANIEL: Not broke down… I remember him wiping a tear.

GWEN: 'Wiping a tear'?

DANIEL: Starting to cry, yeah.

GWEN: Oh no, Daniel, your grandfather wasn't one to cry.

DANIEL: Yeah I seen him. He had a tear when we worked on the car that time, when he promised me I could have it.

GWEN: Well I can't see that myself. I had a cousin, a big man and he had a, oh, a congenitally blocked tear duct, poor devil.

DANIEL No, I was just going 'What do I do now?', and he's there—a bit embarrassing for a young fella, y'grandpa blubbering.

GWEN: Now now.

DANIEL: What?

GWEN: I knew him best and I never saw him cry.

DANIEL: Maybe you didn't but maybe he might have had reasons to cry in front of me.

GWEN: Laugh-cry perhaps.

DANIEL: It was ages after she died, but still, my mum—my real mum was enough to make even Pop cry. That's why he promised me the car: Wendy.

Silence.

GWEN: I remember Wendy running in and she was always busy, busy little girl and she'd be running into the kitchen saying 'Dad, do the space rocket'—I don't know if it was 'space rocket'—but there was this light—'flying saucer'? We bought this light and it wasn't a good buy because the replacement tube was hard to replace as time went on but it looked like a flying saucer see? The little ones said that, I thought it looked more, well it was an elegant sort of thing, and, but, he'd pick her up and fly with her, around the light, Wendy this is. Well the little thing, pretty hair and dress flowing, he was always, always, doing this with Wendy, strong from his work, and this one day she kicked her little foot, kicked her little foot, flying past the the the flying saucer. Well, a great shower of glass and I thought Bill's never going to forgive himself, but she didn't cry and I said, 'Oh your father can do no wrong', because she'd be dark on me if I'd smashed the light and no she kept on laughing and carrying on. 'Oh my father can do no wrong.' Well, talk about laugh.

DANIEL: I've heard that story.

GWEN: Yes.

Doorbell. DANIEL *makes a move to answer it.*

DANIEL: Poor Pop. I don't know how I could of saved her—'specially when Wendy's got a little kid, like me, Wendy had me and she's hooked and must have been doped out of it the whole time, and, yeah, you just take the kid and kick your daughter out. Cut all ties. Take the kid.

GWEN: Well, you were very young, Daniel.

DANIEL: But I remember stuff about my real mother.

GWEN: Yes, but you needn't call her that.

DANIEL: All the yelling.

GWEN: No, you weren't there for that.

DANIEL: Well, must have been because I heard it.

GWEN: No no. You were too young to remember. There wasn't yelling.

DANIEL: Well, no, actually, no, and I only say this because with Mykaela she's four and we have to be careful not to raise our voices or talk about things that she'll repeat.

GWEN: Perhaps.

DANIEL: 'Perhaps'? Not 'perhaps'. Not to be harsh or nothin', Nana, but actually, actually, no. Okay? Not 'perhaps'.

GWEN: Alright, Ducky.

> *Doorbell.*

You better get the door. I'll try to remember the name of that comedian on the television.

> DANIEL *opens the door to* FATHER EZEKIEL, *a Nigerian priest. He wears a clerical collar on his pale blue shirt.*

DANIEL: How y'goin'?

EZEKIEL: Hello. Father Ezekiel.

DANIEL: How y'goin'?

EZEKIEL: I am well. How are you?

GWEN: Who is it?

EZEKIEL: Mrs Houlihan.

GWEN: What on earth…?

EZEKIEL: Hello.

GWEN: Ah. Hello, here's Father. Just in time. This is Peg's boy Daniel. He's promised to take me for a drive later.

EZEKIEL: That is good of him.

GWEN: Did they? Come in. We're making a cup of tea.

EZEKIEL: I am sorry to visit before you have settled.

GWEN: What do you mean?

EZEKIEL: It could have waited.

GWEN: I'm not sure.

EZEKIEL: You are still settling in.

GWEN: The cup of tea, is it?

EZEKIEL: I don't want to get in the way.

GWEN: Yes, well, he's come to help.

EZEKIEL: Your grandson has come to help you.

GWEN: Alright, good. I haven't settled in yet, Father.

EZEKIEL: Good on you, Daniel.

GWEN: Good Daniel, the kettle's in that box.

DANIEL: This one says 'bathroom', Nana.

GWEN: Oh... Take it through.

> DANIEL *takes the box through to the bathroom.*

I only like the stovetop kettle but it's packed, dash it. My daughter, Peg, will be here in a moment and she's bound to know where it is.

EZEKIEL: This box?

GWEN: I haven't got my glasses.

EZEKIEL: It says 'glasses'.

GWEN: Let me see. Alright.

EZEKIEL: Don't you lift.

GWEN: Glassware that means. It's glassware in there.

EZEKIEL: I'll put it...

GWEN: That's a good idea.

EZEKIEL: It is very nice in here, with your air conditioner.

GWEN: Oh, 'air conditioner'. Yes, that was an additional thing we asked for.

EZEKIEL: You will be very happy here.

GWEN: Roasting last night though.

EZEKIEL: I still feel the cold in this part of the world.

> DANIEL *has returned.*

GWEN: Listen, pass the buttons there, Daniel, and I'll turn that air conditioner up; Father's hot.

EZEKIEL: I'm perfectly fine.

GWEN: You're very welcome, Father.

EZEKIEL: Thank you. Yes. People have made me feel very welcome in Queanbeyan: smiles and kind words.

GWEN: Aren't you marvellous?

EZEKIEL: But it is nice to be invited into a home. Thank you for having me. In your home.

GWEN: Fancy no slice to serve. Poor Father, starving like a Biafran.

DANIEL: You sit down, Nana. I'll find the kettle.

EZEKIEL: When they call from the diocesan office, I tell them I do not even have time to be homesick. They know I am busy so they generously gave me this new diary. They have their joke about 'African time' but I do enjoy having this second diary now. I have plenty to do. I celebrated a funeral this morning. Did you know a Mrs Tovey?

GWEN: What's this?

EZEKIEL: A Mrs Tovey.

GWEN: I'm Houlihan.

DANIEL: Nana, do you know Mrs Tovey?

GWEN: Oh yes. She's not very well, Father.

EZEKIEL: I said her funeral this morning.

GWEN: Well, she's in my prayers. You give her my regards, Father.

EZEKIEL: Yes. She had a beautiful service.

GWEN: Oh she always has. Striking, striking woman.

EZEKIEL: Yes. Okay. Yes. The diocesan office has faxed me this 'Proforma House Blessing' which is different to the blessings that I know. Where is the song?

GWEN: She is coming. Peg's just late.

DANIEL: Peg's coming here?

GWEN: He's a good man this one, Father. He arrives out of the blue to see his grandmother's settled in, that she can find what she needs.

EZEKIEL: That is excellent. Excellent, Daniel.

GWEN: Drives a truck. Grandfather drove a truck. His Uncle Frank drove a truck. The family's been carting livestock longer than anyone remembers.

DANIEL: Yeah. But parcels. I deliver parcels.

EZEKIEL: Great. Great.

GWEN: Yes.

EZEKIEL: Great.

GWEN: Yes. And now he'll find my kettle.

EZEKIEL: Mrs Houlihan, I have the blessing which I can follow... and I know a new phrase in Australia which is 'go with the flow'.

GWEN: I see.

EZEKIEL: Do you know that? 'Go with the flow'.

GWEN: Yes I do try to, Father.

EZEKIEL: Yes, prayer with no song is... In Nigeria, prayer is mostly song. [*Passing the blessing*] Here, Mrs Houlihan...

GWEN: Do I have to sign this?

EZEKIEL: Oh no this is just the printout, the fax, that I will follow to bless the house. I thought you might like to see it. It says to 'discuss the blessing first' and someone has added 'after initial chitchat'.

GWEN: But we can wait, can't we, because Peg is coming. Daniel, call your mother.

EZEKIEL: Yes. We can wait. Yes.

GWEN: Daniel, are you calling Peg?

EZEKIEL: It's only that later I have, later, this appointment. I have an appointment at the library. But no, yes. She would like to be here.

GWEN: Peg was going to be here for the blessing. I think Daniel is calling her. She has that many numbers because she's never home, Father. Overcommitted. Volunteers. And I wanted to play tennis and she was going to arrange—

DANIEL: You can talk to her, Nana.

GWEN: What's this? This is a message. Daniel, is that a message?

DANIEL: Leave a message.

GWEN: [*into the phone*] Hello Peg? Peg. Where on earth are you? Father's here waiting and he's terribly pressed for time. [*To* EZEKIEL, *but for* PEG *to hear*] They all live these terribly busy lives, Father. Peg's been meaning to take me to play my last game of tennis.

> GWEN *passes the phone to* DANIEL.

Hang that up for me, Daniel. I was playing tennis once a month until recently.

EZEKIEL: Which is wonderful.

GWEN: Well. Well it's like riding a horse, really, and once you've done it, you never forget and I could probably still ride a horse, I suppose. Drive a car. But the court will go now because the old place is selling and I wanted to get in before Laurie—my son has taken charge and this week it's the trees. 'No if we're gonna sell, all the trees have to come down, Mum.' And I suppose Laurie knows what he is doing, but that's always been hard to judge. No. My husband made the court with chicken wire and one side of the shed and I've pictured myself playing a last game in spite of the fellas lining up with their chainsaws.

EZEKIEL: And Daniel, can't you take your grandmother to play tennis?

DANIEL: What? Yeah. Definitely. Next week, Nana?

GWEN: No, today's the day. The trees come down tomorrow. Peg knows that.

DANIEL: Ah, that's a pity.

GWEN: Yes.

EZEKIEL: I regret that my afternoon is not free. They are letting me use Skype at the library computer. I have booked it, and my mother is travelling at dawn. At my brother-in-law's office at the university in Lagos, there she and one of my sisters can see me when we talk.

DANIEL: This is the internet, Nana.

GWEN: Oh yes.

EZEKIEL: She would be on the bus now. I have scheduled things around my appointment so there is still plenty of time for the blessing, Mrs Houlihan. We can adjust it for your home. 'Go with the flow'. It starts with 'Peace be with this house and with all who live here'.

GWEN: Amen.

EZEKIEL: Yes but, no, we have not started.

GWEN: Alright. Will we give up on Peg? We have Daniel here.

EZEKIEL: Well...

GWEN: People are pressed for time.

EZEKIEL: No no.

GWEN: Daniel wants us to start.

DANIEL: I don't care.

GWEN: He does care.

EZEKIEL: I am happy to wait.

GWEN: I agree. It serves Peg right. Teach her a lesson. Fire away, Father.

EZEKIEL: 'Peace be with this house and with all who live here. Blessed be the name of the Lord.'

GWEN: Amen.

EZEKIEL: 'When Christ took flesh through the Blessed Virgin Mary, he made his home with us. Let us now pray that he will enter this home and bless it with his presence.'

The automatic roller door in the garage is heard opening. Light streams in.

'May he always be here among us; may he nurture our love for each other, share in our joys, comfort us in our sorrows.'

EZEKIEL *stops, the noise of the door has distracted him.*

Someone is joining us?

DANIEL: Nana.

GWEN: What's this?

GWEN *opens her eyes and shifts to see. The roller door halts.*

DANIEL: The garage door opened out there, Nana.

GWEN: Let me see.

GWEN *moves and the garage door is heard again.*

DANIEL: Does Peg have a key?

GWEN: No.

The roller door responds to GWEN*'s movement again.*

Oh, I see, no. Help me up, Daniel.

The roller door stops.

That's. Look there. Blinkin' thing. Take that hoo-haa and hang it on the hook near the pantry.

DANIEL *takes the remote control for the roller door from Gwen's chair. He goes to hang the control but there is no hook.*

Jolly things. Terribly sorry, Father.

EZEKIEL: Not a worry. No worries. 'Inspired by his teachings and example, let us—'

GWEN: What's this?

EZEKIEL: Ah… 'Let us seek to make our home before all else a dwelling place of love diffusing far and wide the goodness of Christ.' Amen.

GWEN: Amen.

EZEKIEL: Now the Scripture is read by a family member.

DANIEL: [*quick to pass* GWEN *her reading glasses*] Here y'are.

EZEKIEL: You read it for us, Daniel.

GWEN: Well that was lovely. Thank you.

EZEKIEL: There's still some more, Mrs Houlihan. Daniel will read the Scripture.

DANIEL: Oh nah, y' reckon?

EZEKIEL: You just read from here.

DANIEL: Ah. Yeah. Alright. Here? Okay. [*Reading*] 'A reading…'— phwa, yeah—'A reading from… from the letter of Paul to the…'

EZEKIEL: The Colossians.

DANIEL: Nup. Can't. You read it.

EZEKIEL: It sounded good.

DANIEL: Hey, mate… Don't make me.

EZEKIEL: No, okay. And. Okay. [*Reading*] 'You are God's chosen race, his saints; Bear with one another; forgive each other as soon as a quarrel begins.' The word of the Lord.

GWEN: [*the response*] 'Thanks be to God.'

EZEKIEL: 'Let us now roam from room to room, offering prayers of intercession.'

GWEN: What's he want?

DANIEL: For us to roam.

GWEN: Rome?

EZEKIEL: Roam with me from room to room. No need to get up, Mrs Houlihan.

> EZEKIEL *and* DANIEL *move to the front entrance.* GWEN *slowly starts to stand.*

'O God, protect our entrances and exits; that those who enter here may know your love and peace. Grant this through Christ our Lord.'

GWEN & EZEKIEL: [*together*] Amen.

EZEKIEL: Are the other rooms through here?

GWEN: Beg y'pardon?

DANIEL: Yeah, mate.

> *By the time* GWEN *stands, the procession has left. She is alone again. She shuffles towards them in silence. The ceremony is soon heard from the other rooms.*

EZEKIEL: [*offstage*] Okay. Now this. Okay. Your bedroom, Mrs Houlihan. 'Protect us, Lord, watch over us as we sleep, that awake we may keep watch with Christ, and asleep, we may rest in his peace.'

GWEN: Can't hear!

EZEKIEL: [*offstage, louder*] 'Grant this through Christ our Lord.'

GWEN: Amen! Show him the sewing room, Daniel.

EZEKIEL: [*offstage*] Oh I'll have to ah… O God, give your blessings to all who… sew in this room… bless… that we may be knit together in companionship.

GWEN: Amen?

EZEKIEL: [*offstage*] Grant this through Christ our Lord.

> GWEN *rests at the door frame and strains to hear.*

GWEN: Has he done the sewing room?

EZEKIEL: [*offstage*] Amen.

DANIEL: [*offstage*] That was the sewing room, Nana. [*To* EZEKIEL] I'll just…

The roller door is heard closing.

EZEKIEL: [*offstage*] This doesn't really cover the garage but I can say: Bless this place… where we park, where we commence our journeys and… Protect us, Lord, as… we take to the highways and byways. Bless us as we reap the soil… with these tools and garden implements. Grant this through Christ our Lord.

GWEN: Amen.

EZEKIEL: [*offstage*] And that is the…

DANIEL: [*offstage*] The spare room.

GWEN: The spare room. Good.

EZEKIEL: [*offstage*] Bless this emptiness, this space, that when we fill it, we make love in it.

EZEKIEL *returns to the kitchen.* DANIEL *follows. They pass* GWEN. *She turns to make her slow journey towards them.*

We will just roam over here… [*Into the refrigerator*] 'O God, you fill the hungry with good things. Send your blessing on us and make us ever thankful for our daily bread. Grant this through Christ our Lord.' Amen.

GWEN: Amen.

EZEKIEL: And we bless a crucifix next.

GWEN: A what?

EZEKIEL: A crucifix.

GWEN: What is it?

EZEKIEL: A crucifix to bless.

DANIEL: Nana, a cross, to bless, in the house.

GWEN: No, it's packed. Goodness knows where. That'll have to wait.

EZEKIEL: Your house is blessed, Mrs Houlihan.

DANIEL: That's it, Nana.

GWEN: That's it?

EZEKIEL: I improvised some of it.

GWEN: Oh, lovely, yes.

EZEKIEL: God bless you.

GWEN: Deep in your heart, tell me, you would like that cup of tea.

EZEKIEL: No, the cup of tea does not matter. Mrs Houlihan, instead of a drive, why don't we take you to tennis?

GWEN: Well, Naomi says get a Fox television, and, I dunno, watch the tennis on television and have a treadmill here to keep exercising, but what is a Fox television?

DANIEL: Satellite television.

GWEN: Well, no, we won't need that, but I like the dancing shows, Father. I know they don't dance how we danced and they spend too long congratulating themselves but when they do dance, yes, I do enjoy the dancing shows on television.

EZEKIEL: I could squeeze in some tennis I think.

DANIEL: Nana—

GWEN: I do like songs that ask me to put my hands up in the air.

Pacharo Mzembe as Father Ezekiel in the 2010 Company B / La Boite production in Sydney. (Photo: Heidrun Löhr)

DANIEL: Father's offered to take you to play tennis.

GWEN: Oh. Do you play tennis, Father?

EZEKIEL: Actually, I have never played. Today will be my first game of tennis.

DANIEL: He'll take you to tennis.

GWEN: Oh. Well. Well that's… I'll drive us to the old house, Daniel will give me a driving lesson on the way, and we three can play a game of tennis.

DANIEL: Nah, I don't have time to play tennis, Nana.

GWEN: Poor Father Ezekiel wants a rally and I'm no Evonne Goolagong. Father, if the ball comes near enough and my racquet happens to be up and it happens to bounce off the strings I'll call that a hit, and I'm happy with that, but, to be quite truthful, I don't return too many shots. But you have to keep active and too many of my friends have stopped. I'm going to get changed. Won't be long, Father. Daniel?

DANIEL: I could drive you in.

GWEN: No no, I'll spin us around there.

EZEKIEL: I have a car.

DANIEL: He has his car, Nana.

EZEKIEL: It's not my car.

GWEN: Go on, give me a driving lesson, Daniel.

DANIEL: I would really like to, Nana—

GWEN: Ah thank you, Daniel. He's made my day now. Take fifty dollars.

DANIEL: What? No. Keep your money.

GWEN: Dive into my purse there, Ducky.

DANIEL: No.

GWEN *is on her way out.*

GWEN: Go on. Fifty dollars.

DANIEL *takes the money.*

Hey listen, I know, 'clipboard' is what the girl from the Roads and Traffic Authority holds. 'Clipboard'. That's it. Father, I'm getting into my tennis gear. 'Put your, put your, put your hands in the air, in the air.'

GWEN *exits.* DANIEL *places the fifty-dollar note back into Gwen's purse on the bench. Silence.*

EZEKIEL: Well it is great to finally be in the company of a young man.

DANIEL: Right.

EZEKIEL: No that's just how it is.

DANIEL: Yep.

EZEKIEL: I am dedicated to my parishioners but, you see, where are all the young men?

DANIEL: Dunno.

EZEKIEL: They do not want to be priests in Australia.

DANIEL: Probably not.

EZEKIEL: No. Do you like football?

DANIEL: Soccer?

EZEKIEL: Yes.

DANIEL: No. Rugby?

EZEKIEL: Okay.

DANIEL: The off-season now.

EZEKIEL: Ah yes. Tennis isn't very popular in Nigeria.

DANIEL: Oh right.

EZEKIEL: No.

DANIEL: Nana's court is pretty terrible.

EZEKIEL: Do you enjoy it?

DANIEL: Not really.

EZEKIEL: Oh well.

DANIEL: Football, is it?

EZEKIEL: Football?

DANIEL: Popular in Nigeria?

EZEKIEL: Yes. Yes. Some people play tennis, I think.

DANIEL: Oh right. You want me to ferret for that kettle, Father? Make yourself at home.

EZEKIEL: Find it for your grandmother.

DANIEL: Yeah, I will, yeah.

EZEKIEL: How long does it take to play?

DANIEL: Tennis? With Nana? All afternoon.

EZEKIEL: Oh.

DANIEL: That's getting her on and off the court. Probably fifteen minutes of play.

EZEKIEL: It is just… I will need to leave to get to my appointment.

DANIEL: I'm not playing tennis, Father.

EZEKIEL: No?

DANIEL: Nup.

EZEKIEL: I am very fond of your grandmother.

DANIEL: Me too.

EZEKIEL: She made slice for my ordination.

DANIEL: Good. Yeah. She always has food. She even puts sultanas in salads. I like it.

EZEKIEL: And she donated one hundred and fifty dollars towards my mother's flight from Nigeria.

DANIEL: Oh yeah?

EZEKIEL: It was very kind.

DANIEL: Yeah. She is kind but she's stubborn.

EZEKIEL: Well…

DANIEL: I don't think she should drive now.

EZEKIEL: We have different rules at home.

DANIEL: The road rules are strict here.

EZEKIEL: We do not tell our elders what to do.

DANIEL: Right. Yeah. How old are you?

EZEKIEL: I'm twenty-eight. I am sorry if before… when I asked you to read…

DANIEL: No worries.

EZEKIEL: If you are a little reticent about the scriptures—

DANIEL: I just, I'm not good at reading out loud. I was that kid at school, the kid with those special pink glasses.

EZEKIEL: This is a good way to look at the world.

DANIEL: Not really. Special reading glasses. You know, actually, go play tennis with her and I could get these boxes going.

EZEKIEL: I am sure she would appreciate that.

DANIEL: Yeah. Work won't matter. Really, I'm a contractor and my truck's in the workshop so… Tell y'the truth: no-one even knows I'm at work today. I just said that to her. I wanted to get going, instead of being stuck here. Still. Still, Nana called me today. She needed me. After a cup of tea I'll get setting up in here for her. See, that's what I'll… The thing you need to keep in mind with me, Father, is I'm the black sheep. Do you say black sheep?

EZEKIEL: No.

DANIEL: No, okay, I'm like the odd one and the breakaway. Not breakaway. I played breakaway for the Queanbeyan Whites. Rugby Union.

EZEKIEL: Tearaway?

DANIEL: I'm a tearaway. I was a tearaway.

EZEKIEL: Well, yes, my parents didn't want the eldest son to join the priesthood but I disobeyed them.

DANIEL: Right. I held up this service station on the other side of town. I was a teenager, wearing my hood all tight on my face but the bloke there goes, 'Come on, Daniel, I know your grandfather'. Queanbeyan's small and I'd been better off getting the bus into Canberra, but you live and learn. Oh well, not that I did learn. But Pop got me to help work on his car with him because of that and, and, I made him cry, and this is only something I've remembered today because, because of the car. Pop was scared I'd go off the rails like my mum.

EZEKIEL: Do you mean Peg?

DANIEL: Wendy. Peg's sister was my mum. Wendy went off the rails. Peg became my mum after that.

EZEKIEL: Okay.

DANIEL: So Pop got Father Mooney to have a word to me about not repeating mistakes no more, not being all yeah, bit of, bit of, oh yeah let's try that, not like, only because, at that age, and you have to, y'know?

EZEKIEL: Not really.

DANIEL: Yeah.

EZEKIEL: You mean drugs?

DANIEL: No. Well. Nothing bad but.

EZEKIEL: What are they like?

DANIEL: They weren't for me.

EZEKIEL: Did Father Mooney pray with you?

DANIEL: Don't think so. Gave me a cold drink and we had a chat.

EZEKIEL: A caring man.

DANIEL: I remember it 'cause it was my first beer. When I say Nana shouldn't be driving like… there was a bloke here before, Father, and Nana's clipped his ute and I had to come sort it out. She had a little prang. That's why she shouldn't be drivin'. Shouldn't be, Father.

EZEKIEL: That has worried you.

DANIEL: Nah. Just, nah. I mean threatening an old lady at her home…

EZEKIEL: He threatened her?

DANIEL: By hanging around. And he would've hit her up for money. It doesn't take much for that cheque book to come out. Nah, we shrugged it off. Nothing, it was nothin'. I wish she hadn't pranged and put me in that position, that's all.

EZEKIEL: Okay. Okay.

DANIEL: Yeah.

EZEKIEL: Okay.

DANIEL: Yeah. I did do like ecstasy, like once. It wasn't as good as anyone reckons.

EZEKIEL: What is ecstasy?

DANIEL: That's a tablet you take, Father. Yeah.

EZEKIEL: Thank you for sharing things with me, Daniel.

DANIEL: No worries. Look I did, I would've done ecstasy three times. Yeah. I'm telling you the weirdest things, Father.

EZEKIEL: Because a little courage can say, 'Jesus, forgive me'.

DANIEL: Yeah. I regret I never said thank you to Mr Bollard because he gave me a job at the servo after the hold-up—people are good like that—and I'd have a little whiff in between customers, trying to rebel, at the bowser, trying to get hooked but I never got hooked. It's all a bit lame. Yeah, but I'm alright now. Now I just keep to myself.

EZEKIEL: Yes?

DANIEL: Yeah.

EZEKIEL: Yes. I see in Canberra, just over in Canberra, these great boulevards but people keep to their houses. Nigerian streets are full.

DANIEL: Right. And, yeah, so my marriage is crumbling a bit. But I can fix it.

EZEKIEL: It is important that you do.

DANIEL: Yeah. I will.

EZEKIEL: There is too much divorce here.

DANIEL: It won't be divorce. Nah.

EZEKIEL: Good.

DANIEL: I didn't do anything to the bloke outside.

EZEKIEL: Okay.

DANIEL: Nah.

EZEKIEL: Do you still congress with your wife?

DANIEL: I, yeah, we talk things over. Is that what you mean?

EZEKIEL: Because there is more to life than sex.

DANIEL: Beg y'pardon?

EZEKIEL: There is much more to it.

DANIEL: You don't do it.

EZEKIEL: What's that?

DANIEL: Nothing.

EZEKIEL: Were you unfaithful?

DANIEL: No. With Bel. We just disagree. It's just time apart. She threatens —says she'll move to Forbes, four hours drive away to Forbes, where her family is, family that she hates, and take my trailer and everything. And. She'll take our daughter with her.

EZEKIEL: Don't let her do that.

DANIEL: Nup. I won't. I won't let her.

EZEKIEL: Will you say a prayer with me, Daniel?

DANIEL: Well… yeah… if you want me to, Father.

EZEKIEL: If you want to.

DANIEL: I don't want to.

EZEKIEL: Then we won't.

DANIEL: I should have… The bloke out front. Can't go around. Old lady by herself. I saw a, there was a little chance, and I could have, it was a chance just to hold that bloke's face. I could have taken his face like that. I knew if I took the, his face, and held it with the bottom of his, of my, hand, under his chin and the, the fingers hooked in there, his eyes, I could have just held him there, if he'd moved he would have been hurting himself with my hand. I could have had him like that.

EZEKIEL: But you didn't?

DANIEL: No I didn't.

EZEKIEL: Good.

DANIEL: Restraint, Father. I held back.

EZEKIEL: I think that is… Because what, what would you have achieved with violence, Daniel?

DANIEL: A little bit of blood.

EZEKIEL: Yes.

DANIEL: Hurting him.

EZEKIEL: Hurting another man.

DANIEL: I was in control of myself, Father. I wanted to look after Nana. Pop would've wanted that.

EZEKIEL: Maybe you should come and play tennis.

DANIEL: You need to get going.

EZEKIEL: No no.

DANIEL: I could have just squeezed at his face so hard. Hurt the... I would have have hated to have done that only because at the end I seen his kid in the car, a little kid there in his Spiderman costume looking so scared of the yelling, all camouflaged in the seat. Nana didn't see the kid but explains why the guy was a bit, car hits you, baby on board, not baby, little boy on board. Explains him going off at her. I saw the kid and lucky I did, Father, well lucky I didn't do what I wanted to do to his old man.

Something is heard bouncing on the roof.

EZEKIEL: Something on the roof, was it?

DANIEL: Something up there?

EZEKIEL: I thought...

DANIEL: Possum.

EZEKIEL: Possum?

DANIEL: Maybe a possum around here.

EZEKIEL: Oh.

DANIEL: But not during the day. Nocturnal, they are. Yeah. And sometimes I put extra hours on my time sheet, Father. Sometimes that's what I do. I will for today more than likely, Father, if I think I can get away with that, I will. One or two.

EZEKIEL: Can I say a prayer now? I'd like to.

DANIEL: Yeah, no worries, mate.

EZEKIEL: I'll say a prayer over you.

DANIEL: Right. Yep. Won't stand in your way.

EZEKIEL: I'll lay my hands on you.

DANIEL: Yeah. Go on.

Water runs down the windows.

EZEKIEL: 'Our Father who art in heaven—'

DANIEL: I know it.

EZEKIEL: 'Hallowed be thy name. Thy kingdom come.'

DANIEL: [*simultaneously*] 'They will be done.'

EZEKIEL: [*simultaneously*] 'Thy will be done.'

DANIEL & EZEKIEL: [*together*] 'On earth as it is in heaven.'

DANIEL: [*simultaneously*] 'Forgive...

EZEKIEL: [*simultaneously*] 'Give us this day our daily bread; And forgive us our trespasses as—

DANIEL & EZEKIEL: [*together*] '… we forgive those who—

EZEKIEL: '… Trespass against us and lead us not into temptation but deliver us…'

DANIEL & EZEKIEL: [*together*] '… from evil.'

EZEKIEL: 'Through Christ our Lord.'

DANIEL: Too easy.

EZEKIEL: 'Amen.'

DANIEL: Amen. Cheers. Okay. I'm not… I won't… I won't put extra hours on my time sheet today. They pay me for doing nothing half the time anyway. Don't have to lie.

Something bounces on the roof again.

EZEKIEL: Maybe children playing with a ball. Maybe their ball is on the roof.

DANIEL: I should go check. No-one lives around here yet.

> DANIEL *leaves through the side door.* FATHER EZEKIEL *remains by himself in Gwen's house.*

> [*Offstage, to* PEG, *some distance away*] Oi! Oi! What're you…? Weird, you are. That's stupid. Bloody stupid. Nah. Take a look at yourself. Nah. I said, take a look at yourself. Yeah.

> DANIEL *comes back in.*

EZEKIEL: Alright?

DANIEL: It's my mum.

EZEKIEL: Peg?

DANIEL: Yeah. Yes. Peg. Peg's putting balls in the gutters.

EZEKIEL: Is she?

DANIEL: She is.

EZEKIEL: Why?

DANIEL: Bushfires.

EZEKIEL: Okay.

DANIEL: It fills the gutters with water in case there's a fire. I don't know if Nana's done the best thing moving out here. I dunno.

> PEG *enters. She wears a nurse's uniform.*

PEG: What are you doing here, Daniel? Mum's got no money for you.

DANIEL: Y'what?

PEG: Father's here? Oh wonderful. Has Mum asked you to bless the house?

EZEKIEL: She did, yes.

DANIEL: He's just done it.

PEG: You've done it?

EZEKIEL: Yes.

PEG: You've done it without me. Oh, that's alright. Yes. Alright then.

PEG *exits.*

EZEKIEL: Oh.

DANIEL: God.

EZEKIEL: Everything alright there?

DANIEL: I dunno. Yeah.

EZEKIEL: I hope I haven't caused any problems.

DANIEL: Nah. Wouldn't think so. She's just a bit...

EZEKIEL: What?

DANIEL: She's all... y'know.

EZEKIEL: You must not disrespect them, Daniel.

DANIEL: Who?

EZEKIEL: These people in your life. You need them.

DANIEL: Do I?

EZEKIEL: I think your mother is upset.

DANIEL: She's alright. This is just what Peg does.

DANIEL *opens the door to find* PEG *halted nearby.*

What are you doing standing just there? Are you going now?

PEG: No.

DANIEL: You're standing right there.

PEG: Am I?

DANIEL: Yes. What are you doing? Come back in.

PEG: I'm just about to do the fire thing.

DANIEL: You've done it. Come back in.

PEG: Don't try to correct me, Daniel.

DANIEL: Come back in. Bloody... Just...

DANIEL *gets* PEG *inside.*

PEG: Oh well, I feel dreadful, Father: I've missed the blessing. It must be my fault. Mum must have got the time wrong. It's my fault. I would have loved to have heard you sing. Did you hear Father sing, Daniel? Was it glorious?

EZEKIEL: I didn't sing.

PEG: We all love your beautiful voice, Father.

EZEKIEL: Thank you.

PEG: Daniel—

DANIEL: I just came here to help Nana.

PEG: Oh thank you. Good.

DANIEL: With the— To unpack.

PEG: Good. Okay. How's little Mykaela?

DANIEL: She's good.

PEG: I bet she's grown. If Bel ever needs—

DANIEL: Don't.

PEG: I was only—

DANIEL: Not interested.

PEG: It's a sight here, Father. What a sight? It is thoughtful of you, Daniel, but we've paid someone to unpack for Mum. You needn't have driven to the end of the earth.

DANIEL: D'you worry about her on these roads?

PEG: No. Why?

DANIEL: Just…

PEG: That's the last thing I need on my plate: worrying about Mum's car upturned in the river. Your grandmother's an excellent driver, Daniel.

DANIEL: Okay.

PEG: I said I would unpack but others insisted that I mustn't. We've got unpackers coming in. I said I'd be overjoyed to work on it through the night and around my classes, but I've been told. Oh and I… I'm going to pin this on the fridge. Mum is going to think it terribly amusing: like a little girl, pinning her school assignment on the fridge. I'll be asking for an all-day-sucker next.

EZEKIEL: What is it?

PEG: Oh you used to get lollypops that you could suck all day, Father. Years ago.

EZEKIEL: Oh okay. And what have you got there?

PEG: Oh this? No I don't really want to make a show of it. I got an assignment back from my course. I've gone and got water on it from the hose now. I drive out to Canberra for classes and I've got a distinction.

EZEKIEL: Congratulations, very good.

PEG: Oh. No. I have got one High Distinction but that was in an elective that I chose for myself so that doesn't really count.

EZEKIEL: No that is very good.

PEG: I wish I put it in a better plastic sleeve. Water's in it. Never mind, yes. I was storming heaven over this assignment, Daniel. I'm new to it all, Father, and I had such nerves. I know I would have cried if I'd got anything less. Maybe that's why the tutor marked it up: she probably knew.

EZEKIEL: Oh well you should be proud.

PEG: Oh, thank you. Thank you. No. 'Where's the other ten percent?' Dennis and I used to encourage the children when they got constant good marks and we'd say 'Oh well, next time it will be one hundred percent'. But no I do know where I lost marks and that's important. Now, I wonder... Mum used to have dear little magnets on the old fridge. Have we seen them?

DANIEL: No.

PEG: Oh she had lovely little ones on the Kelvinator. Places she'd been. I remember one from Batemans Bay. Oh I do hope they haven't been hurled.

DANIEL: Some packing tape here.

PEG: Oh no that will mark the fridge.

EZEKIEL: Could you clamp it in the, that, door somehow?

PEG: Oh that's a very good suggestion, Father, yes. Or I could pop it inside but the ink might run when the paper thaws.

DANIEL: Look, no, Peg, you just... with the packing tape.

PEG: But this fridge is brand new, Daniel.

DANIEL: [taking PEG's assignment] Yeah they stick stuff on it at the shop: Energy rating sticker.

PEG: Give it back, Daniel, please. No look I'll just leave it here where she'll find it later and it'll, sort of, it'll be a bit of fun. She'll remember us bringing school reports home. It was my dear older brother Frank— 'Eternal rest grant unto him, O Lord...'

PEG & EZEKIEL: [together] '... and let perpetual light shine upon him.'

PEG: Amen. Thank you, Father. My older brother Frank got the most gold stars. He needn't have misspent a career transporting livestock with his father, should have been something more, but loyalty got the better of Frank. I'd never say that to Dad— 'Eternal rest grant unto him, O Lord...'

PEG & EZEKIEL: [together] '... and let perpetual light shine upon him.'

PEG: Mum's doing a slice here is she? She's coming. Everyone let's all act normal.

> GWEN *enters. She is dressed for tennis replete with a white visor and little pompoms on her socks.*

GWEN: I'm in my tennis gear.

PEG: Oh not tennis, Mum.

GWEN: Where were you?

PEG: It was my fault, Mum. We clearly got the time wrong.

GWEN: How?

PEG: I just…

GWEN: We tried to call. We all gave up on you in the end, Peg.

PEG: Oh well, I don't have reception out here. There's no coverage out here, Mum. Not for mobile telephones. Father, I am so desperately sorry.

GWEN: Well, there is that saying, Peg, about how if you make people wait they'll spend the intervening time calling to mind all your faults.

PEG: I don't know that one, Mum. Why are you dressed for tennis?

GWEN: I am dressed for tennis.

PEG: Why?

GWEN: I'm going to play it in a moment.

PEG: Oh no, Mum, I've been putting it off.

GWEN: Father's taking me.

PEG: Father hasn't got time for that.

EZEKIEL: Well…

GWEN: Is it still cold out?

PEG: No it's blistering. Father's too generous.

GWEN: He can speak for himself.

PEG: I'd like to be there in case there's any wrong-footing.

GWEN: Yes, doubles would be lovely.

PEG: So many people shatter their hips, Mum.

GWEN: Alright.

PEG: It's why I wanted a matte finish on the floors here.

GWEN: Alright.

PEG: But I was overruled.

GWEN: There are handlebars by the bath, Peg.

PEG: Mum's fiercely independent, Father. Mum, I've followed the Rural Fire Service's leaflet for blocking the gutters. You'll survive a fire-storm now, Mum.

GWEN: That's kind. I know it was one of your things.

PEG: Yes, I told the others that we'd get that done because it was one of the objections I had to buying a place like this out here, way out here.

GWEN: Thank you, Peg. They were thoughtful objections.

DANIEL: Is anyone else cold?

PEG: Mum, I went and visited Marcella Puccinelli.

GWEN: Oh yes.

PEG: Father's seen me up there.

EZEKIEL: Where's that?

PEG: The Home. Up at the Home.

EZEKIEL: Oh yes.

PEG: Yes. Because I'm the Eucharistic Minister up there and so I swing in and see some of the old faces. But you must go visit dear Marcella Puccinelli, Mum.

GWEN: Yes I intend to.

PEG: She's up there and she looks very relaxed. They look after them very well. She looks like a fallen bird. A little fallen bird. These wispy patches of white hair. Chirping away. Not chirping really. 'You're like a fallen bird from a dear little nest, Mrs Puccinelli.' And she 'mmmm' something back. They know there's someone in the room—not that she'll recall it's Peggy Colderick née Houlihan, who asked her son to a Marian Club dinner dance, years back, before I met my late husband Dennis, but she'd have some sense of a presence in the room, of colours and shapes. 'This is like looking through a mottled window at the world you'll soon farewell for the stained glass of heaven.' That's what I say. I say that to them. A little bird. Fallen from the nest. Trying to get through the glass. Oh you must get up there, Mum.

GWEN: I do intend to. It's the parking.

PEG: It is the parking. Well there's no time for sitting.

DANIEL: You're standing.

PEG: I'll finish making this slice for you, Mum.

GWEN: I've given up on that.

PEG: [holding a new baking dish] Heck, Mum, what's this? What are these new…?

GWEN: We decided on that stuff.

PEG: No, Mum. What's Naomi done? Those lovely old baking dishes?

GWEN: Old as the hills.

PEG: But the quality, Mum.

GWEN: Falling apart.

PEG: No-no-no-no the dear little pattern on them, Mum.

DANIEL: Peg, calm down.

PEG: What? 'Calm down'? 'Calm down'.

GWEN: Leave the slice: oven's broken. I'll get a man in.

PEG: Oh, Mum, but this is supposed to be new. This has to work, Mum. The light's on. The fan, Mum. This is fan-forced, Mum.

GWEN: I've read the booklet.

PEG: Let me see the booklet. Excuse me, Father.

GWEN: No. I'll only get confused. I'll reread the booklet. I'd like to do it myself.

PEG: Don't get someone in. Promise me you won't waste your money.

GWEN: I won't. Just leave it for now. Daniel wants to have a look at it for me.

PEG: Daniel? Oh well that's… Good, Daniel. That's. The old oven worked perfectly fine. Naomi Naomi Naomi jolly well rifling through it all. I take that back: my sister's not heartless. Just remiss.

GWEN: I kept the old enamel kettle. It's somewhere.

PEG: Father, cup of tea?

EZEKIEL: No thank you, Peg.

DANIEL: Is it freezing in here?

PEG: Tennis? What am I thinking? I have to get to work. I'm due at work shortly. There'll be no tennis for me.

GWEN: That's a pity.

PEG: Well my work is important.

GWEN: Of course it is.

PEG: It's very important to me.

GWEN: No-one's disputing that.

PEG: And why would they? Listen, my work is very important. It is to me. I can't be late.

GWEN: You get going then.

PEG: Oh, there we go, usher me out the door. Next you'll need a little bag for your ticket stubs. No that fell flat because I was being a smartalec. I've got time to do some unpacking here before the unpackers arrive.

GWEN: No, Laurie cancelled that. It was too costly.

PEG: I said I was prepared to do it.

GWEN: He's doing it himself.

PEG: Where are we now? In a sea of boxes. And I've gone and taken extra shifts to save for my busy exams up ahead.

DANIEL: Why is it so cold?

GWEN: Daniel, look for a box in there marked 'racquets'.

PEG: With the erosion of the tennis court, Mum, are you sure?

DANIEL: Are you cold, Father?

EZEKIEL: A little chilly.

PEG: Fix it, Daniel, quickly.

GWEN: Shall we go to tennis?

PEG: I'll categorise your pantry.

GWEN: 'Categorise the pantry'?

PEG: You'll want particular things at eye level.

GWEN: There's nothing wrong with my eyes.

PEG: I know you're particular about particular things at eye level.

GWEN: Don't, Peg.

DANIEL: Peg…

PEG: [*moving past* EZEKIEL *to the pantry*] [I will just] pop through there, Father.

GWEN: Come sit down.

DANIEL: She wants you to sit down, Peg.

PEG: Barely a thing unpacked.

DANIEL: But just sit down.

PEG: 'Sit down'?

DANIEL: I hate it. I hate it. I hate it.

PEG: What's the matter now, Daniel?

DANIEL: I just hate it when you don't stand still all the time.

PEG: The pantry, Daniel.

DANIEL: This is why we all can't bear to be around you.

GWEN: Daniel, carry a chair over to your mother. If she can't stand still at least she can sit down as she sorts the pantry.

PEG: I can close the door if I'm in the way.

> DANIEL *has the air conditioner remote.*

GWEN: Listen, what are you fiddling with there?

DANIEL: It's got too cold.

GWEN: Wait. Let me see. I'll adjust it.

DANIEL: I've just done that.

GWEN: Hand it here and I'll—

DANIEL: I've put it to—

GWEN: No, but you need to select the setting. That isn't what we want. Here. That's an 'icon'. Click two three. That will 'swivel' now. Terribly good, this thing. Watch it. Swivels. See?

DANIEL: Yeah but it cools down too fast.

GWEN: I've fixed it. Don't touch it; I'll be out of sync... Ducky.

EZEKIEL: Very pleasant.

GWEN: Daniel you'll find the racquets near the linen cupboard. I saw them there. A box clearly marked 'racquets'.

>   DANIEL *leaves to get the racquets.*

PEG: Mum, has Daniel been a nuisance?

GWEN: Oh no. I was delighted to see him. I called Daniel and his eyes lit up and he said 'Oh no I'll take the afternoon off and see your new place' and now he'll play tennis.

EZEKIEL: We should probably 'get a wriggle on', Mrs Houlihan.

GWEN: I didn't catch that, Father.

EZEKIEL: 'A wriggle on'.

GWEN: Yes?

EZEKIEL: A wriggle on for tennis.

GWEN: Yes.

PEG: Oh blow it, I've thrown the tennis balls on the roof. I'll need a ladder and gloves. I'll have to climb up there and get them down.

>   GWEN *sits.*

GWEN: No we have other balls in there with the—

>   *The phone rings.*

PEG: Quick grab the—

GWEN: I'll get it.

PEG: Mum, I'll—

GWEN: I can get it.

>   DANIEL *returns with a box marked 'tennis'.*

PEG: Daniel—

GWEN: Help me up.

PEG: Get her up, Daniel.

GWEN: I've got it.

PEG: I'll answer it for you, Mum.

GWEN: No. Let me answer it.
PEG: Quick, Daniel, the phone before it... Daniel.
DANIEL: You right, Nana?
GWEN: Quite right.
PEG: Help her along, Daniel.
GWEN: I'm alright.
PEG: Help her, Daniel.
GWEN: I'm alright.
EZEKIEL: Shall I?
PEG: You'll miss the phone, Mum.
GWEN: I won't miss it.
EZEKIEL: I can grab it.
PEG: Answer it, Daniel.
GWEN: No no, Peg. Please. Please. Just. Please.

The phone stops ringing.

PEG: It's stopped, Mum. The phone has stopped ringing now, Mum.
GWEN: People know to call twice.
DANIEL: Probably just a telemarketer.
EZEKIEL: Ah yes.
PEG: They won't ring again. Can we retrieve the number, Daniel?
GWEN: But they know to call back.
PEG: It might have been my Mark calling from Berlin or Deirdre in Tokyo
    without the money to call twice.
DANIEL: They could get real jobs.
PEG: Oh but he's a video artist, Daniel.
DANIEL: That's right.
PEG: And she's a blogger now. They'll be wishing you all the best, Mum.
    So kind of them, Mum. First day in the new house, Mum.
EZEKIEL: Perhaps you could get a cordless.
PEG: It is a cordless, Father, only Mum hasn't worked out how to use it
    yet. She keeps it on the charger. It is a cordless.
GWEN: It will ring again.
EZEKIEL: Surely.
DANIEL: It was just a telemarketer.
GWEN: It will be someone from the family. They all call.

They wait for the phone to ring.

PEG: Mine have been instilled with a beautiful sense of family.

Silence. The phone does not ring.

EZEKIEL: Actually, I have just been given a new mobile phone. It's called
a—

The phone rings. GWEN *soon answers it.*

GWEN: Hello? Yes. Hello. Yes. Yes. Yes. That's good, Laurie.

PEG: It's Laurie. Ah.

GWEN: Yes. 'Moving along'.

PEG: It must be moving along.

GWEN: What did they say?

PEG: The real estate.

GWEN: I see. I see. Yes.

PEG: [*to* GWEN] What did the real estate say?

GWEN: Oh. Already?

PEG: An offer. It will be another meagre offer. They turned it in at auction.
It was all a mistake. Bridging finance through the roof.

GWEN: Yes.

PEG: Laurie's doing everything wrong. Seemingly deliberately. We've
always thought that about Laurie.

*Melissa Jaffer (left) as Gwen and Sue Ingleton as Peg in the 2010
Company B / La Boite production in Sydney. (Photo: Heidrun Löhr)*

GWEN: Yes.

PEG: Dad used to say, in a funny way, 'Oh that Laurie, he is destined to
fail at everything he attempts'. Dad had a wicked sense of humour.
A turn of phrase. 'You're a great disappointment to me, Laurie': in a
very amusing voice.

GWEN: Yes but they'll dismantle it tomorrow.

PEG: [*to* GWEN] Which mantle, Mum?

GWEN: Yes. No. I see. Yes. Yes. I was going up today. I know that. Well.
I've been trying to get *someone* to play a last game. Yes. No. Well.
Yes. I know. Yes. You'd better go. She is. Yes. Peg's here. Yes. And
Father Ezekiel. Yes. Father Ezekiel. Yes. Father Ezekiel. The... Yes.
No, just the three of us. Hmmm? Bye. Bye now, Laurie. God bless.
[*Finished on the phone*] I think he's gone.

> GWEN *passes the phone to* DANIEL.

Hang that up for me, dear.

PEG: And? What did he have to—?

GWEN: He's got a fine from the council for cutting down the trees.

PEG: For heaven's sake.

GWEN: But the men have dismantled my court to get the trees down.

PEG: Oh that blinkin' Laurie.

GWEN: I thought this was tomorrow. No more tennis. What a fool am I?

> GWEN *takes off her tennis hat.*

EZEKIEL: Is, ah, there are the council courts?

DANIEL: Nana? I'll book you in at the council courts.

GWEN: No no, it's done now.

PEG: Fancy moving it forward. It's like Laurie gets a thrill from putting
people out.

GWEN: He sounded terribly deflated.

DANIEL: Yeah someone oughta, bloody, let the air out of him.

PEG: Oh, Daniel. That's, yes. Wicked. You've inherited that wit. Did you
hear it, Mum?

GWEN: What'd he say?

PEG: Someone should let the air out of Laurie.

GWEN: Of?

PEG: You said he was deflated, Mum, and Daniel said 'Yes someone
could puncture Laurie because he's so overweight'.

GWEN: Oh. He's quick.

PEG: Terribly funny, yes. Father, Laurie has put on weight since his retirement. And that's a worry for heart attacks. Rosemary Stanton says that. This band of fat around a man's middle is what brings on the heart attacks.

GWEN: Your brother Frank was slim.

PEG: Frank was unlucky. Laurie's digging his grave with a dessert spoon.

GWEN: Sorry, Father, about the tennis.

EZEKIEL: Don't mind me.

GWEN: You had your heart set on it.

EZEKIEL: It is quite alright.

GWEN: I'd like a cup of tea.

PEG: I'm looking for the kettle. I want to know it's survived.

DANIEL: I've already looked there.

PEG: I'll have to get on to Saint Anthony.

EZEKIEL: [*to* PEG] Let me lift that.

PEG: Thank you, Father. [*To* GWEN] You'd like to get changed again, Mum?

GWEN: I'll manage.

PEG: I need to get on the road: you're fine; you don't need a hand getting changed, do you?

GWEN: Sometimes… If only Frank were still here.

PEG: Or Dad.

GWEN: [*to* PEG] Your brother Frank would've soon calmed things down.

PEG: 'Eternal rest grant unto them, O Lord…'

PEG, EZEKIEL & GWEN: [*together*] '… and let perpetual light shine upon them.' Amen.

    LAURIE *enters, mobile phone in hand. He is dressed for business.*

GWEN: Jove. How's he done this?

LAURIE: Mobile phone, Mum. Magic.

PEG: Laurie. Oh. Laurie. We were just… Laurie, do you know Father Ezekiel?

EZEKIEL: We have not met. Hello.

LAURIE: Pleased to meet you, Ezekiel. You've done your voodoo for Mum then?

PEG: Laurie? Laurie is only acting the goat, Father. Laurie wanted to be on radio when he was a boy. He wanted to tell jokes for a living. It didn't work out.

LAURIE: Something like that, Peg. [*To* DANIEL] And how are you, Gangsta?

DANIEL: That's not my name, Uncle Laurie.

LAURIE: Didn't you want to change your name to that? Sing rap songs. And we all laughed.

DANIEL: Yeah. Not anymore.

PEG: Daniel, will you go in and grab Mum's slippers?

LAURIE: [*distributing house keys*] Mum, there are some spare keys. Peg, you'll want a set.

PEG: Oh no no, I'm too frightened I'll set off the alarm. You just hang onto them and I'll always call in advance to see Mum's in, like you've done.

GWEN: You don't get reception out here, Peg.

PEG: Mum wanted to play tennis, a last game, Laurie.

LAURIE: She can't now.

PEG: And I only wish I took her up sooner.

LAURIE: You should have done.

PEG: Laurie, I can see it in your eyes, you've been through an ordeal. Having those fruit trees come down and getting the fine… You're deflating.

LAURIE: No. I'm disputing the infringement notice. I'm writing to the mayor. I knew his father once and it can go to the *Queanbeyan Age* if needs be. They'll have a clever headline about it if it comes to that. I'll think one up and suggest it.

GWEN: Like what, Laurie?

LAURIE: Something about… these… trees. I don't have it yet.

PEG: Oh well, I'm glad it's you and not me, Laurie. I'm glad I wasn't included in any of the discussions in the end. The tiles aren't to my taste and it's so unnecessary, to me it seems extravagant, to have a spare room.

LAURIE: It's what Mum wanted.

PEG: And it does sound hectic getting a fine. But how sad to see the fruit trees go.

LAURIE: Well, the motel man over the back fence appreciates the size of the land now. He's enticed: knock it all down and extend for serviced apartments. You'll all thank me soon. Mum's not used to business and this is my skill set. We've all heard of people taking advantage.

Tricksters knock at the door. You know, and the money Mum's dished
out for people over the years—

PEG: Daniel, she would have left the slippers by the bed. And her dressing-
gown, please.

GWEN: I don't need that, Peg.

LAURIE: Someone'd come for a handout and they got money no matter
what damage they were lumping on Mum.

PEG: Oh but Laurie those trees. Father, we all played in these lovely
countless trees as children.

LAURIE: We didn't. They were so toxic from Dad spraying, it's a wonder
we didn't all drop dead [given] all the stewed fruits we ate from them.

PEG: Laurie always had a second helping but no I remember clearly
playing in them and laughing and nonsense and there was no poison
that got me.

GWEN: Your father never had a sick day in his life.

PEG: No we're strong stuff. Imagine Dad still pruning trees at his age
before he dropped off his perch. One fall can change everything.

GWEN: He hadn't had so much as a Disprin till he was ninety.

PEG: But, dear man, he went in such peace.

LAURIE: Kicking and flailing at the nurses: he didn't know where he was.

PEG: Oh no, Laurie, that's not how it was. Remember? Remember the
chaplain came in and said 'Oh hello there, Bill, you're going with
God now'.

GWEN: 'You are going to God, Mr Houlihan' was what he said.

PEG: I don't recall the exact words, Father.

GWEN: That's what he said. Your father found great solace in that, Laurie.

PEG: God has been good to us, Father. And if it weren't for my dear
brother Frank's heart attack he'd be here laughing with us today.

GWEN: We've had our trials.

PEG: Mysterious ways.

GWEN: What's that?

PEG: Mysterious ways, Mum.

GWEN: God does. Yes.

PEG: He does. God's been good. And when my husband's feeding tube
failed one last time, I had my faith to carry me— I've told you this
story, Father.

EZEKIEL: You have. God bless him.

PEG: Watching Dennis gasping those last breaths, I rejoiced about where my husband was going. I pray every day for thanks, Father.

EZEKIEL: So do I.

PEG: 'Eternal rest...

PEG, EZEKIEL & GWEN: [*together*] '... grant unto him, O Lord, and let perpetual light shine upon him.' Amen.

DANIEL: And Wendy.

PEG: Oh and Wendy, Daniel. No-one's forgetting Wendy. My baby sister, Father. Wendy.

    Silence.

GWEN: I remember Wendy running in here and she was always busy, busy little girl and she'd be running into the kitchen saying, 'Dad, do the space rocket'. There was this light.

PEG: No, Mum. That was me with the light. You keep getting that wrong.

GWEN: I don't think so, Peg.

PEG: It's wrong. Wendy wasn't even born then.

GWEN: Up at Crawford street.

LAURIE: Don't look at me.

PEG: Dad stopped doing it because I smashed the globe.

LAURIE: Does it matter?

PEG: I'm sorry. . You tell it however you like.

GWEN: It's very easy to criticise.

DANIEL: It does matter.

PEG: Forget it.

DANIEL: No it does matter. It does. And look, what you said before, Mum... About Nana being 'an excellent driver', she's not.

GWEN: Ducky.

DANIEL: Not anymore.

PEG: Where's this come from?

DANIEL: Nana had a prang before.

GWEN: Daniel.

PEG: Mum? Were you hurt?

LAURIE: What happened, Mum?

GWEN: Such silliness.

LAURIE: We're insured. How much damage, Mum?

GWEN: I don't think it even happened.

LAURIE: Well we'll dispute it. Do the police know?

DANIEL: No. There's no need for that. I dealt with the guy.

LAURIE: You did?

DANIEL: Nana was frightened.

PEG: Oh Mum.

GWEN: Please, Daniel.

DANIEL: And she phoned me.

LAURIE: Don't go doing that, Mum. We've all got mobiles. I'm leaving my card by your phone.

> LAURIE *places a business card near the phone.*

DANIEL: I dealt with the guy.

LAURIE: And I'll follow it up.

DANIEL: No. I dealt with the guy. He was an easygoing bloke. Barely a mark on his ute. The damage was on the Special.

LAURIE: I should follow it up.

DANIEL: Nothing more to be done. But Nana shouldn't be driving.

GWEN: Rot.

LAURIE: You shouldn't be driving, Mum.

From left: Grant Dodwell as Laurie, Melissa Jaffer as Gwen and Sue Ingleton as Peg in the 2010 Company B / La Boite production in Sydney. (Photo: Heidrun Löhr)

DANIEL: And I'd like to have Pop's car.

LAURIE: I bet you would.

GWEN: It's my car.

DANIEL: Nana, I only want you to be safe.

GWEN: And that'll be why you came in a taxi today, Daniel.

DANIEL: No, because, Nana, my truck's in the workshop. Nana? It is. I swear.

GWEN: I see.

LAURIE: Don't worry, Mum. He's not getting the car.

PEG: No-one is.

DANIEL But, Uncle Laurie, it's not for you to— Grandad said I could have it.

LAURIE: He what?

DANIEL: Do you know that?

LAURIE: No. I don't.

DANIEL: Peg? You must know that.

PEG: Daniel, Mum needs her car. How will she get the things she needs? Who will run her about?

DANIEL: But you know he said that to me.

PEG: I don't know what he said.

DANIEL: I won't forget it: seeing Pop cry.

LAURIE: Ha. Ha. That'll be the day. The cranky old so-n-so. Ha.

DANIEL: Yeah, no. He did. Wasn't ever cranky with me.

LAURIE: No. You might have got special treatment or something, Daniel, but Dad didn't go around giving gifts. And we'd have it in writing if he wanted you to have the car. God knows he never threw anything out. I found a box, this is funny, a box labelled 'padlocks that no longer have keys'. Depression era see, Father. Couldn't turf a bloomin' thing.

DANIEL: But maybe he said something to me he didn't write down.

GWEN: He wouldn't have, Daniel. He never said it.

DANIEL: But how can you know? I remember what he said. And you'd all know why he'd cry, he cried, in front of me. Nana? Wendy. Wendy's why he promised me the car.

LAURIE: Here we go.

DANIEL: What?

LAURIE: Here we go. Don't go sniffing around for Wendy's share, Daniel.

DANIEL: I've never asked for nothing.

LAURIE: She put all that up her arm. 'Cash injections'. Even Frank made that joke.

PEG: We're not like that. No. No and Mum knows all I want left for me is a few lovely things from the kitchen: something Naomi can't replace like that funny old cheese bell.

DANIEL: Are you trying to provoke me, Uncle Laurie?

EZEKIEL: I will have to make my way to the library. I should probably get myself on the road.

PEG: Father, how lovely it's been.

GWEN: God bless you, Father. You don't want to see us carrying on. It's embarrassing, Father.

EZEKIEL: No no, in fact I have felt my most homesick being in this home today.

PEG: Well that's good.

EZEKIEL: And Daniel, could I give you a lift back into town?

DANIEL: Yeah. That might be a good idea, Father. Just. Pop stood next to the car and he starts bawling about his regrets. He went, went red in the face, and went on about Wendy... about how much he regretted going over to Wendy's this day, to our place, and dragging me away from her.

LAURIE: Okay. You've got your story straight. You see how this works, Mum?

DANIEL: People think I don't know. But Wendy had me in my terry-towelling shorts and the red gumboots that made me look like Astro Boy. She gave me that stuff. We have a photo of that outfit. And Pop, and you, Nana, came and there was yelling.

GWEN: There was not.

DANIEL: I know all this and, you know what, I forgive you. I'm over it. Whatever. I don't need anything from you. Whatever. I've got my work and I've got my kid and... doesn't matter what any of you say or do for me. Not you. Not you. Not you. I know what Pop said, clear as day, the promise he made about the car, but be it on your conscious, Uncle Laurie.

PEG: Conscience. You mean 'conscience', Daniel.

DANIEL: What? What?!

LAURIE: Daniel, I don't think he did say that. I don't think Dad said any of that.

DANIEL: Why not?

LAURIE: Because Wendy was busy with a needle in her vein—

GWEN: Laurie!

LAURIE: She sent some boyfriend with his tight black jeans and rat's tail—

GWEN: Don't—

LAURIE: She had this drop kick dump you at the front gate.

GWEN: No.

LAURIE: We all remember that. Too well. And don't you dare lump my mother with your lies.

> DANIEL *grabs* LAURIE's *face. They all talk over the top of each other.*

EZEKIEL: No.

GWEN: Hey now.

PEG: Daniel, don't.

GWEN: What's…? My house. My house. Not in my house.

EZEKIEL: Let go of his face, Daniel.

LAURIE: Let go.

From left: Sue Ingleton as Peg, Pacharo Mzembe as Father Ezekiel, Nathaniel Dean as Daniel and Grant Dodwell as Laurie in the 2010 Company B / La Boite production in Sydney. (Photo: Heidrun Löhr)

PEG: Let go of your uncle's face, Daniel.

EZEKIEL: Daniel. Come on now, Daniel.

PEG: Is it hurting you, Laurie?

LAURIE: Yes.

DANIEL: Stop moving, Uncle Laurie.

LAURIE: Let go of my face.

DANIEL: No I won't.

PEG: Please.

DANIEL: I won't let go of your face.

EZEKIEL: Stop. Stop, Daniel. Stop.

GWEN: You'll never be invited back here, Daniel. Never.

> EZEKIEL *pulls* DANIEL *away and restrains him.*

PEG: You alright, Laurie?

LAURIE: That can't happen.

EZEKIEL: Peace.

LAURIE: Can't do that, Daniel.

EZEKIEL: Peace now.

PEG: Laurie, will I get some frozen beans for you? In case your face swells.

DANIEL: Are y'bleeding, Uncle Laurie?

LAURIE: Am I?

GWEN: He's okay.

LAURIE: Where's the blood?

EZEKIEL: There is no blood.

GWEN: Show me.

LAURIE: I'm bleeding, am I?

GWEN: I can't see any blood.

EZEKIEL: We'll go, Daniel.

LAURIE: There's a little bit of blood there.

GWEN: Is that blood? That's sweat. You're alright, Laurie.

LAURIE: I don't know if I am.

PEG: Freezer's empty. I think you'll be okay, Laurie.

GWEN: There there, Laurie. Brave soldier.

EZEKIEL: Come with me, Daniel.

LAURIE: [*to* DANIEL] You shouldn't have done that.

PEG: He knows it was a terrible thing to do. We needn't go on about it, Laurie.

GWEN: [*to* LAURIE] Especially when it was your own doing.

LAURIE: Ha. That was my own doing, was it, Mum? Ha.

GWEN: Absolutely. Brought it on yourself.

PEG: A shame you have to get going, Father.

GWEN: Do us all a favour, Laurie—

LAURIE: Mum—

GWEN: You haven't got anything intelligent to say; keep your fat gob shut.

DANIEL: No. No he's right to say what he said. Is it true?

PEG: It doesn't matter.

DANIEL: [*to* PEG] Yeah, na, but it's true? Wendy… Wendy did that?

PEG: Daniel, I made you the Astro Boy gear.

DANIEL: Yeah?

PEG: Yes, dear. For your birthday, after you'd come to live with us.

DANIEL: Alright. Alright. Uncle Laurie. Laurie?

LAURIE: No, you keep, keep away from me.

GWEN: [*to* DANIEL] You children have all got such wonderful teeth. No fighting, Daniel.

DANIEL: Yes, Nana.

GWEN: You stay away from Laurie. He's hardly worth it.

PEG: Laurie's only trying his best, Mum.

GWEN: Ha.

DANIEL: [*to* LAURIE] I'll pay you. I'll pay for the car. Uncle Laurie, you'll only sell it. Let me buy it.

GWEN: Laurie's trying his best is he?

DANIEL: [*to* LAURIE] Whatever, name your price.

LAURIE: [*to* DANIEL] Well. Well, we ought to get it valued.

DANIEL: Not hard to do.

LAURIE: Not too hard no. I'll get it valued.

PEG: Hang on.

DANIEL: I know a bloke. I can put you in touch.

LAURIE: I'd get an expert to look at it.

DANIEL: Whatever it's worth is what I'll pay.

PEG: Now just hang on. Mum's astute and she needs to be in on this. Mum's fiercely independent. Aren't you, Mum?

GWEN: What am I?

PEG: Fiercely independent.

GWEN: Oh yes. And I need my car. No-one's getting their hands on that car. Try as they might.

LAURIE: No it's a sensitive thing, Mum, that's understood but we don't want you in danger and we don't want anyone giving you a hard time.

GWEN: Thank you, Laurie.

DANIEL: What's your number, Uncle Laurie?

LAURIE: I'll give you my card.

DANIEL: I thought you'd retired.

LAURIE: [*his business card*] I got these made up.

EZEKIEL: That is a handy thing to have.

LAURIE: You can have one too, Father. There you are. And pass that one to Daniel.

EZEKIEL: Thank you. Where'd you get them done?

LAURIE: Out in Fyshwick. There's a place. My wife Bambi wanted the cats on them. That wasn't my idea but she has a website to promote. There y'are, Peg.

PEG: I don't need one, Laurie. I have your number in my directory and we're all told to stop wasting paper these days or the ozone will blow up.

GWEN: What's blowing up?

PEG: Nothing, Mum.

GWEN: The car is perfectly roadworthy.

LAURIE: Mum, I'm not going to let you drive anymore. This prang is the end of the road. I'm forbidding you. It's too dangerous. I'm getting rid of the car right now.

GWEN: But, Laurie, I won't let you take it. I will not. No. Because it's mine. It's not yours yet. You can't. I won't let you.

LAURIE: Mum, you be reasonable.

GWEN: If someone took my car, I'd never forgive them.

LAURIE: Hey now, we've been through it and no-one likes the idea of another test. Peg, Mum won't sleep if she knows there's a test. The girl bullies you, Mum, and that's because you're not safe in that big old thing.

GWEN: Buy me a small car. When the house sells. It's my money. I'll call Naomi and she will arrange it.

LAURIE: She doesn't want you driving either.

GWEN: Father, you tell them they can't.

EZEKIEL: Mrs Houlihan, if you are not safe maybe you should trust that your children know best.

GWEN: No. Where are my keys? I want my car keys.

PEG: Mum, sit down now.

GWEN *searches for her car keys. She moves faster than she is ever likely to move again.*

GWEN: I want my keys. They're my keys. Your father bought that car. Where are my blasted keys? I need my car. Don't take it from me, Laurie. No. No. No. Please, Peg.

LAURIE *takes Gwen's car keys from her handbag.*

LAURIE: You were never going to pass the next driving test anyway, Mum.

DANIEL: I'll pick you up, Nana. I'll take ya to things. I'll take ya to Woollies.

GWEN: You have your truck. Don't take my car.

DANIEL: I'm gonna make it look real excellent, Nana. I wanna fix it up. I'll restore it like new, Nana. You watch me get it perfect for you.

PEG: Shit.

PEG *sits for the first time in the play.*

GWEN: [*mishearing*] What's that, Peg?

PEG: Shit.

LAURIE *and* DANIEL *leave for the garage.*

LAURIE: Daniel, let's have a look at it. I think we can work out a price.

DANIEL: Yeah. There's a bit of work to be done on it actually, Uncle Laurie.

LAURIE: [*offstage*] Be a bit of a collectors' item.

DANIEL: [*offstage*] Yeah. Maybe. Still see a few of them around but.

Silence.

PEG: That air conditioner is a nuisance. Blows straight onto your chair. I'm getting your gown.

GWEN: Wendy left you a bag of clothes in there.

PEG: Beg your pardon?

GWEN: Wendy's put a bag of clothes in there. You'll see it in the spare room. Things she doesn't need anymore.

PEG: Naomi has?

GWEN: Yes.

PEG: Oh well I'll have to phone Naomi and thank her for that.

PEG *exits. Silence.*

EZEKIEL: My mother will be just coming into Lagos now. The roads are safer further in.

Silence. PEG *returns with Gwen's slippers, gown and Naomi's David Jones bag filled with clothes.*

PEG: Oh she's terribly amusing. She's put… Mum, she's written 'hand-me-ups' on here. I'll have to call her.

PEG *drapes the dressing-gown on* GWEN's *shoulders.*

GWEN: I don't want that.

PEG: … nor a chill, Mum, in your tennis skirt with that blizzard blowing.

GWEN: Pass the [air conditioner] buttons then.

But PEG *passes the belt for the gown.*

PEG: Naomi buys very good quality, Mum. They'd be dear: these clothes. I bet that new phone was costly.

GWEN: Yes. I think it's fairly state-of-the-art.

PEG: Yes Naomi said that. Did you get a coffee in Canberra together?

GWEN: Yes. All very pleasant out there.

PEG: Some good coffee in Queanbeyan now. Someone said. The old convent finally got bought. Things happen there. Art classes. A coffee shop. Been meaning to…

GWEN: There's a chap playing piano at David Jones.

PEG: Oh, you would have enjoyed that.

GWEN: No, he wasn't on.

PEG: Oh that's a pity.

GWEN: Yes.

PEG: She would have put it on her David Jones card. She told me to get one but I'm never there and I can't work out how to redeem the points. No.

EZEKIEL: Excuse me.

EZEKIEL *exits to look at the car.*

GWEN: Naomi's buying me a treadmill but I said 'no'.

PEG: No she's not.

GWEN: I know what she said.

PEG: It's a new treadle for your Janome. I have to pick it up, way out in bloody Belconnen.

GWEN: No need to swear.

PEG: I only wish Naomi would make more than a flying visit.

GWEN: She goes to tremendous cost to visit me. All the way from Surfers Paradise, Peg. And she's terribly busy.

PEG: The car is going to go, Mum.

GWEN: We'll see.

PEG: It's gone. I'll take you to Mass each week. You're not to worry about that, Mum. We do 'stress' in one of my units. It comes up in tutorials all the time. It's the real killer. You'd be fascinated by the scientific things they know and the things I'm learning, Mum.

GWEN: Yes. I would be.

PEG: I'm the one who'll be expected to drive you. That's what is happening now.

GWEN: I won't let them.

PEG: Mum, this is what's happening now.

GWEN: I don't know what Laurie thinks he is up to out there.

PEG: That spare room here is for me, isn't it, Mum.

GWEN: It's a lovely big spare room.

PEG: I know you've been talking to Laurie about that room.

GWEN: It's just for people who want to stay.

PEG: Naomi stays in a hotel out at Civic.

GWEN: Well she gets 'deals' with these things.

PEG: Mum, they want to install me here as your full-time carer, don't they?

GWEN: You're good to me, Peg. You are good to me. I do know that, Peg.

PEG: They know they can depend on me.

GWEN: Thank you, Peg.

PEG: You'd love some of the fashion on campus, Mum. Lovely young figures they have. I worry about what to wear some days. But no-one's looking. A lovely girl who dresses like Jenny Kee invited me to study with her circle but I couldn't bear their music. How they concentrate, I do not know. And the woman who lectures us is so clever for her years. I find it inspiring out there, Mum. I'm the happiest and the strongest I've ever been.

GWEN: Good, Peg.

PEG: That's why I'm going to say 'no' to you, Mum. I have to say 'no'. I came here today and stood out there and I seized up. I saw this place and I imagined you in here. And I hate these tiles. I just hate them. I froze out there and that's why I missed the blessing. I was so looking forward to it, Mum, but I just went cold. You called my phone and I let it go to message bank. But don't you worry, Mum, you can rely on me. And, look, see, when I do my shopping I'll collect the groceries you need.

GWEN: I'd like to do my own shopping, Peg.

PEG: Sometimes I will take you.

GWEN: I'll shop for myself.

PEG: Sometimes I won't be able to take you, Mum.

GWEN: Peg? I thought you had your heart set on that spare room.

PEG: No. You didn't. You had no reason to think that. We've never even discussed it, Mum.

GWEN: I know what I thought.

PEG: I just… I still hear Sister Mary Robb in the middle of my Leaving year: 'Oh no, Peggy Houlihan, your father's called. You're to move back home to Queanbeyan to help your mother with the younger children and the housework.' From that phone call and through all the children and then caring for Dennis… I never got my ticket. All my brothers and sisters, they got their ticket. And I won't let you do it again. You know why I'm saying 'no', Mum.

GWEN: Then go in there and stop Daniel taking my car from me.

PEG: Like fun. I can't tell him what to do. He resents me.

GWEN: He needs you.

PEG: He knows. He knows I haven't… I've struggled to love him like my other children.

GWEN: You mustn't say that, Peg. No mother thinks that.

PEG: Yes, some do. I tried so hard to be his mother. I've always said yes to you, everything you've asked.

GWEN: It's a funny way you're going about that today, Peg.

PEG: You always have to have the last word, Mum, but now I'm—

The men re-enter. DANIEL *has the car keys.*

You can listen to this, Laurie. I've told Mum I won't be moving into the spare room. I know that's your plan. That spare room is for storage. If there's anything you and Naomi haven't thrown out it can be stored in there. I doubt there's much. The catalogues and 'hey this is on special, Peg', that's all Naomi seems to keep. I know Dad hoarded too much, all the balls of string and the rubber bands on the door handles, but Naomi threw out his handkerchiefs. I wanted to keep just a little hanky of Dad's. He always had a hanky in his overalls pocket here. I told her I wanted to pin it on my blouse at the funeral. I wanted to wear one like a rosette. Laurie? You hear, Laurie? And that old wheelbarrow that I thought if I go and do a course in folk art I could make a really beautiful thing and, Laurie, you said it 'smells too bad'.

LAURIE: Blood'n'bone tends to, Peg.

PEG: Not to me. Reminds me of Dad and you threw it out, Laurie. Oh and weren't you keen on this cul-de-sac way out here?

LAURIE: You done yet, Peg?

PEG: I'm talking to you, Laurie.

LAURIE: My sister could talk under water with a mouthful of wet cement, Father.

DANIEL: Uncle Laurie, you listening to Peg?

PEG: It's alright, Daniel.

LAURIE: Peg, you haven't even heard what we want to do for you.

PEG: Oh yes? What's my consolation prize, Tony Barber? That was sarcastic. I hate sarcasm. I'm sorry everyone.

LAURIE: Peg, you've taken on too much.

PEG: Actually, no, I'm very good with stress, thank you.

GWEN: You never dealt with Dennis properly. You went straight from sitting by a hospital bed to enrolling in nursing.

PEG: Which is what I wanted. This is not everyone let's look at Peg for a long time and and and make her feel inadequate. That's not the name of this, here, today.

LAURIE: Look, Peg, Naomi and I want to do something for you. You won't have to work; there'll be a contribution made to the household here and you'd be entitled to an allowance.

GWEN: And you could move from that hovel where you live.

LAURIE: And you know if it were within the realm of possibility, yes, Bambi and I would consider shifting across but with Bambi breeding the Burmeses now… Besides, like Naomi and Graeme, we own— You'd have no rent to pay, Peg. That should be made clear.

PEG: Where is this 'contribution' coming from, Laurie? You? Naomi? I'm not your Vinnies' bin, thank you very much.

LAURIE: From the estate.

PEG: Mum happens to be alive, Laurie.

LAURIE: Dad's will. The executor has strict duties; I'm to hold money from the house sale in trust.

PEG: You? Why?

LAURIE: Yes, me.

PEG: I wasn't told about that.

LAURIE: 'Held in trust by the eldest son' to provide for his mother's care and wellbeing.

PEG: He meant Frank.

LAURIE: It's logical, Peg. This is what we all want to do for you. And if you still want to finish the uni stuff, then why don't we look into doubling the sewing room as a study? Peg, you'd be doing the right thing by Mum.

PEG: I thank everyone for their concern but other arrangements will have to be made.

LAURIE: So you'll abandon your mother?

PEG: I have to get to my shift in a moment.

LAURIE: We're never gonna get her into a nursing home, Peg.

DANIEL: Uncle Laurie, mate, Peg said 'no'. Peg's allowed to say 'no' for once.

LAURIE: Come on, Mum. You defend me here.

GWEN: Well... Well all I can say is God's squeezing his hand tight on me. He's made some joke of my life. You all have. You're robbing me of my car. You wretch, Laurie. Putting your mother on the bus! What would your father say?

LAURIE: I dunno, Mum, sounds like he'd break down and have a good old cry.

GWEN: Your father should be here for this, because I can't take it. And what would your brother Frank think of this mess, Laurie? God's taken the wrong one first.

LAURIE: Is that right, Mum?

PEG: She didn't mean to say that, Laurie.

GWEN: Say what?

LAURIE: I can take care of myself, Peg.

GWEN: Listen, what is it I've said?

LAURIE: That you wanted me to go instead of Frank.

GWEN: Laurie? No. I didn't say that. I never meant that. I said God took your father before me and I don't know why. Why is he punishing me?

LAURIE: I just have to… I ought to call the estate agent before the close of business and…

GWEN: Laurie? I've hurt you, Laurie.

> GWEN *goes to* LAURIE.

LAURIE: No you haven't…

> LAURIE *hides his face on* GWEN'*s shoulder. Everyone watches.* LAURIE *is crying.*

I'm going to just pay that council fine. It was my fault.

> LAURIE *exits. Silence.*

GWEN: Do you think he'll be alright driving? Do I need to call him, Father?

EZEKIEL: I don't know.

PEG: I think just leave him be for a night, Mum. He'll come back to you.

> *Silence.* DANIEL *dials his mobile.*

DANIEL: Hang on. I'll… Listen to this, Nana. Hang on. You'll like this.

> *Silence.*

[*Into his mobile*] Hi it's me. Oh yep. Later. I just wanna— [*To* GWEN] Sorry. Just a minute, Nana. Bel's putting— [*Into his mobile*] Yep. I don't know. Can't you do that in Forbes? I didn't call for…

PEG: [*to* DANIEL] Why's she in Forbes?

DANIEL: [*into his mobile*] No. Could you put Mykaela on? No I wanted to speak to— Yeah. I, yep. Not now. Bel, I know but please not now. Put Mykaela— Bye. 'Kay. Bye. [*To* GWEN] I can put it on loudspeaker. Hear? She's… You can hear her coming.

GWEN: What is it?

DANIEL: Mykaela on the phone.

GWEN: Oh yes. Lovely.

DANIEL: Mykaela. This is Daddy. Say 'Hello Daddy'. And Nana's here.

CHILD'S VOICE: Hello Daddy.

GWEN: Is it a recording?

PEG: No she's on the phone, Mum.

DANIEL: Say hello.

PEG: It's a loudspeaker.

DANIEL: And Peg. Peg's here.

GWEN: Dear little thing.

DANIEL: Do your thing for your Grandmas. Go on, Mykaela.

EZEKIEL: You can hear her breathing.

DANIEL: [*to Mykaela*] Only naughty girls are shy.

PEG: Oh leave her.

GWEN: Darling thing. She should visit more. Bring her around.

DANIEL: I will yeah.

PEG: [*to* DANIEL] Yes. Good. Do.

> *Mykaela sings a racy pop song for them.*

DANIEL: She loves this one. She knows it. Off Video Hits.

> *They applaud when Mykaela finishes the song.*

Good girl.

GWEN: She's precious.

PEG: Darling thing. When will you bring her around?

DANIEL: Say 'bye-bye', Mykaela. Bye-bye. Hang up. Hang up.

> *They all say goodbye. Mykaela doesn't.* DANIEL *hangs up his phone.*

Yeah. Thought you'd like that. Good, hey.

PEG: Yes.

GWEN: Oh yes.

EZEKIEL: Great.

DANIEL: Yeah. Cheer you up. Alright then.

PEG: You going?

DANIEL: Yeah. Goodbye, Nana. I'll come and…

GWEN: Good, dear.

DANIEL: Yeah. Bye.

PEG: Everything's alright with you and Bel, Daniel?

DANIEL: Yep. Bye Father. It was nice to meet you, mate.

EZEKIEL: Ah, yes, okay, Daniel. Peace.

DANIEL: See yez.

PEG: God bless, Daniel.

DANIEL: Bye… Peg.

> DANIEL *leaves with the car keys.*

> *Throughout the following* PEG *removes* GWEN*'s tennis shoes and replaces them with the slippers.*

PEG: I'd better… just save you bending…

The garage door is soon heard opening. DANIEL *backs out the car. He triggers the garage door to close. The car is driven away. The garage door closes and shuts off the sounds.*

[*Continuously*] Get these on you… How do these—?

GWEN: You—

PEG: Do I—

GWEN: That's it.

PEG: Alright. A bit…

GWEN: They are a bit…

PEG: Yes.

GWEN: That's got it.

PEG: Well. I'm already going to be late.

GWEN: You fly then, Peg.

PEG: I will, yes. Father, you'll have to excuse me [for] dashing off to work. Sorry again for missing your blessing, Father. Your singing was beautiful. I know it would have been beautiful if I'd been here.

Clockwise from left: Melissa Jaffer as Gwen, Pacharo Mzembe as Father Ezekiel and Sue Ingleton as Peg in the 2010 Company B / La Boite production in Sydney. (Photo: Heidrun Löhr)

EZEKIEL: Thank you.

GWEN: And, Peg, don't feel you have to sleep here tonight.

PEG: Tonight?

GWEN: No. I don't want you to worry about me.

PEG: Mum, you had a good sleep here last night?

GWEN: Oh yes. It took me back to when I was a girl actually.

PEG: Good.

GWEN: Yes.

PEG: You'll settle in here, Mum.

GWEN: I lay there thinking, 'No, I won't sleep with the light on'. And I didn't because that would have been wicked waste.

PEG: You know I'm not going to stay here, Mum.

GWEN: But in time…

PEG: Mum…

EZEKIEL: Peg, what I will say is, is, sometimes we are called on to make sacrifices.

PEG: I know that too well, Father. Wait till I get the other slipper on, Mum.

EZEKIEL: I think you do. I know you do. And I know you love your mother. It is not my place to impose but what I would like to say about this is: because you love your mother, when the time comes, you will not let that spare bedroom remain empty.

PEG: Father…

EZEKIEL: I promise you that you will find great peace in your choice.

PEG: Yes, Father. Mum, promise me you will get up to see Marcella Puccinelli.

GWEN: Yes, Peg.

PEG: And there are other people you'll know up there. You should see them before they go.

GWEN: Yes. I do intend to do that.

PEG: Oh the kettle. I still have to—

GWEN: No no. Leave it. I won't be having tea until the morning.

PEG: I'll be here in the morning, Mum. I'm coming back tomorrow and I'll get this unpacked. I can miss one tutorial; others do. And I have Saturday off or I've, ah, I'll ask to swap for a late, so I can be here then. God bless, Father.

EZEKIEL: God bless.

PEG: Mum. God bless, Mum.

> PEG *considers the spare keys that Laurie has left. She takes her set.* PEG *exits without Naomi's bag of clothes. Silence.*

GWEN: It's ah... Oh it's like... Ah... What's it like? Reminds me of... Ah. No. I've forgotten.

EZEKIEL: What did you forget?

GWEN: Hmmm?

EZEKIEL: What was it you forgot?

GWEN: Yes. Oh well.

EZEKIEL: It will come back to you.

GWEN: I clean forgot what I was going to say just now.

EZEKIEL: Never mind.

> *Silence.*

GWEN: You must miss your mother, Father.

EZEKIEL: She will be nearing her destination.

GWEN: Your mother?

EZEKIEL: Yes. I think they are going to bid me home. They always wanted the eldest son to stay and provide but I disobeyed them. I must get to the library.

GWEN: Why don't you come and visit again, Father?

EZEKIEL: Why don't we make a time?

GWEN: Yes?

EZEKIEL: To come back and see you.

GWEN: Will you come and see me?

EZEKIEL: Yes.

GWEN: I think that's a splendid idea.

EZEKIEL: I'm just seeing...

GWEN: Yes. What's this?

EZEKIEL: My diary. Are you free next Monday?

GWEN: Yes. Yes. Yes.

EZEKIEL: Oh, yes, I need to... What about Tuesday?

GWEN: That day, Father? Yes.

EZEKIEL: Yes. I do have... Why don't I call you from the Presbytery. I will call to make a time. It is just that I now have two diaries and I'm yet to transfer, Mrs Houlihan.

GWEN: Call me Gwen, dear.

EZEKIEL: Yes. Okay.

GWEN: And do come again, dear.

EZEKIEL: We will make a time for next week.

GWEN: Oh grand. Grand.

EZEKIEL: Is it too hot in here for you now? I think the air conditioner has got very hot.

GWEN: The temperature?

EZEKIEL: It's warm.

GWEN: 'Reverse cycle'.

EZEKIEL: Are you getting too hot?

GWEN: If it's cold I'll have this on.

> GWEN *pulls the dressing-gown on.*

EZEKIEL: You wouldn't want it too hot at night. Could I look at it for you? Shall I adjust it?

GWEN: Are you cold? Or are you hot?

> GWEN *examines the air conditioner control and makes some adjustments.*

EZEKIEL: I thought it a bit hot.

> GWEN *looks to the air conditioner.*

I think if you…

> *Unsatisfied that her adjustments have registered,* GWEN *goes to the wrong panel in the wall and hits a button.*

Okay?

> GWEN *looks to the air conditioner. Perhaps now it is following her commands.*

GWEN: Good.

EZEKIEL: I will come and see you again.

GWEN: Good.

EZEKIEL: If you would like the sacrament of reconciliation, I will come and collect you and we can go to the church. Be at peace with God, Mrs Houlihan.

GWEN: I see. I get terribly weary in the afternoons.

EZEKIEL: You have a rest then.

GWEN: Now I don't want you to be late.

EZEKIEL: Shall I sit with you a little bit longer?

GWEN: You go, get to your appointment, dear.

EZEKIEL: Yes. Alright. Thank you, Mrs Houlihan. God bless. No no, I'll
    let myself out.

>   GWEN *follows* EZEKIEL.

GWEN: God bless, Father.

EZEKIEL: God bless.

GWEN: Ta-ta for now, dear.

>   GWEN *locks the door behind him. She collects all the things she'll
>   need; the phones and the controls are placed within reach of her
>   chair.*

>   *After a long period of stillness, seated in her chair,* GWEN *starts
>   the staggered process of dozing. Dip by dip, she ebbs into shallow
>   sleep.*

>   *The home alarm sounds!* GWEN *quickly computes where she is and
>   what is alarming her. The alarm. The alarm. The alarm.*

>   *The standing regime repeated,* GWEN *moves as fast as her frame
>   of ninety years will carry her. She approaches the control panel on
>   the wall. She examines it and enters a code. The alarm continues.*
>   GWEN *tries again. She cannot shut it off. How can it be wrong?*

>   GWEN *journeys to her reading glasses and back to the panel and
>   makes another failed attempt. Again. Again.*

>   GWEN *goes to the phone but she can't hear the dial tone over the
>   noise. She finds Laurie's business card but puts it aside. She finds
>   Peg's university assignment, glancing over it before returning to
>   the alarm panel with her purse. She shifts Naomi's bag of clothes
>   to get in closer.*

>   GWEN *holds her driving licence and strains to read the date of
>   birth before firmly pressing each of the four digits again.*

>   *We stay with* GWEN *for a painful duration and her many attempts
>   to end the nauseating decibels of the alarm.*

END OF PLAY

www.currency.com.au

Visit Currency Press' website now to:

- Buy your books online
- Browse through our full list of titles,
  from plays to screenplays, books on
  theatre, film and music, and more
- Choose a play for your school or amateur
  performance group by cast size and
  gender
- Obtain information about performance
  rights
- Find out about theatre productions
  and other performing arts news across
  Australia
- For students, read our study guides
- For teachers, access syllabus and other
  relevant information
- Sign up for our email newsletter

The performing arts publisher